W9-AXS-659

EXCEPTIONAL WEALTH

CLEAR STRATEGIES TO PROTECT AND GROW YOUR NET WORTH

MARK M. TEPPER, CFP®

GREENLEAF
BOOK GROUP PRESS

This publication is designed to provide accurate and authoritative information in regard to the subject matter covered. It is sold with the understanding that the publisher and author are not engaged in rendering legal, accounting, or other professional services. If legal advice or other expert assistance is required, the services of a competent professional should be sought.

Published by Greenleaf Book Group Press
Austin, Texas
www.gbgpress.com

Copyright ©2018 Mark Tepper

All rights reserved.

No part of this book may be reproduced, stored in a retrieval system, or transmitted by any means, electronic, mechanical, photocopying, recording, or otherwise, without written permission from the copyright holder.

Distributed by Greenleaf Book Group

For ordering information or special discounts for bulk purchases, please contact Greenleaf Book Group at PO Box 91869, Austin, TX 78709, 512.891.6100.

Design, cover design, and composition by Greenleaf Book Group

For permission to reproduce copyrighted material, grateful acknowledgment is made to the following:

From "Confessions of a Former Financial Advisor: 5 Things I Didn't Tell My Clients," by Erik Carter. From *Forbes,* December 13, 2015. All rights reserved. Used by permission and protected by the Copyright Laws of the United States. The printing, copying, redistribution, or retransmission of this content without express written permission is prohibited.

Excerpt from *Capital Without Borders: Wealth Management and the One Percent* by Brooke Harrington, Cambridge, Mass.: Harvard University Press. Copyright © 2016 by the President and Fellows of Harvard College.

Excerpt by Rory Vaden from RoryVaden.com. Copyright © by Rory Vaden. Reproduced by permission of the author. roryvadenblog.com

Charts from "Putting a value on your value: Quantifying Advisor's Alpha." © The Vanguard Group, Inc. Used with permission.

Cataloging-in-Publication data is available.

Print ISBN: 978-1-62634-456-3

eBook ISBN: 978-1-62634-457-0

Part of the Tree Neutral® program, which offsets the number of trees consumed in the production and printing of this book by taking proactive steps, such as planting trees in direct proportion to the number of trees used: www.treeneutral.com

Printed in the United States of America on acid-free paper

17 18 19 20 21 22   10 9 8 7 6 5 4 3 2 1

First Edition

TreeNeutral®

To my family, my clients, and the Strategic Wealth Partners team—my heartfelt thanks and appreciation. I'm glad to have all of you as my partners in this journey.

CONTENTS

YOU'RE WEALTHIER THAN YOU REALIZE

What is wealth? It's a word with endless definitions. More to the point, wealth means different things to different people. So as you begin reading and you ask yourself, "Am I wealthy?" don't forget to ask, "What does wealth mean to me?" Your answer will have a lot to do with the value you get from this book.

To illustrate, here's a parable about wealth and life that I really like. You might be familiar with it, but even if you are, it's worth reading again:

> An American investment banker was at the pier of a small coastal Mexican village when a small boat with just one fisherman docked. Inside the small boat were several large yellowfin tuna. The American complimented the

Mexican fisherman on the quality of his fish and asked how long it took to catch them.

The Mexican replied, "Only a little while."

The American then asked why he didn't stay out longer and catch more fish. The Mexican said he had enough to support his family's immediate needs.

The American then asked, "But what do you do with the rest of your time?"

The Mexican fisherman said, "I sleep late, fish a little, play with my children, take siestas with my wife, Maria, and stroll into the village each evening where I sip wine and play guitar with my *amigos*. I have a full and busy life."

The American scoffed and said, "I am a Harvard MBA, and I could help you. You should spend more time fishing and, with the proceeds, buy a bigger boat. With the proceeds from the bigger boat, you could buy several boats. Eventually you would have a fleet of fishing boats. Instead of selling your catch to a middleman, you would sell directly to the processor. Then you could open your own cannery. You would control the product, processing, and distribution. You would need to leave this small coastal fishing village and move to Mexico City, then L.A., and eventually New York City, where you would run your expanding enterprise."

The Mexican fisherman asked, "How long would this all take?"

"Fifteen or twenty years."

"But what then?" asked the Mexican.

The American laughed and said, "That's the best part. When the time is right, you would announce an IPO and sell your company stock to the public and become very rich. You would make millions!"

"Millions? And then what?"

The American said, "Then you would retire. You could move to a small coastal fishing village where you would sleep late, fish a little, play with your kids, take siestas with your wife, and stroll into the village in the evenings where you could sip wine and play guitar with your *amigos*."

The point of the story isn't to paint the fisherman as a saint or the businessman as a greedy stereotype. Each represents a valid choice: to be a small, independent businessperson or a capitalist entrepreneur. The message is that the Mexican fisherman already has a life that gives him everything he needs; in his mind, he's wealthy. It may not be the American businessman's version of wealth, but that doesn't matter.

The word *wealth* means something different to everybody. For some, wealth is all about the numbers on the balance sheet. For others, it could be about what your money empowers you to do, such as live your lifestyle without fear of having to scale back when you retire. True wealth is about having the freedom to enjoy the things in life that are most important to you: family, leisure time, volunteering, and so on. So how do you know if you're wealthy? You're wealthy if you have the resources to live the life you want to live, without compromise.

It doesn't matter what anyone else's definition of wealth is. Yours is the only one that matters. Helping you achieve your optimal version of wealth is the reason I wrote this book.

YOU'RE PROBABLY WEALTHY

Do you have a net worth between $1 million and $5 million? Congratulations! You're doing very well. You occupy a stratum of the American economy ranging from about the top 10 percent to the top 3 percent. If you're over $5 million—say, with a net worth of $10 million—you're really in the rarified air: the wealthiest *0.7 percent* of American households.[1] But even with that kind of wealth, do you really think of yourself as "rich"?

If not, you have plenty of company. According to a 2013 report from investment bank UBS, only 28 percent of Americans with $1 million to $5 million in assets consider themselves wealthy.[2] Why? Well, there might be a few psychological principles at work here. The theory of *relative deprivation* says that no matter what we have, we're more likely to feel that it's inadequate when we compare it with what someone else has. When compared with someone else's $10 million portfolio, $2 million in assets may not seem like much. Another fundamental aspect of our psychology is that most of us adjust quickly to a new status, so it becomes our new set point—our new normal. Think back to your first salary raise. It's likely that you were thrilled about it . . . for a while. But before long, your lifestyle adjusts, and you become just as dissatisfied with that level of income as you were with the previous one. You start looking toward the next milestone.

All this would seem like a behavioral curiosity were it not for one sobering fact: Not realizing their own wealth leads some investors to pursue poor and sometimes costly financial advice. Shockingly, there are people who earn $250,000 or more per year, with a net worth of more than $1 million, who insist on calling themselves "middle class." You may be smiling because you're one of those people, but before we move on, let me set you straight about your wealth. If you have a household income of $250,000 and investable assets of $1 million, you are in the top *4 percent* of this country's population. By definition, that is not middle class. It is not upper-middle class. It isn't even upper-*upper*-middle class. You are *wealthy*. If you're going to get the most out of this book, it's important that you begin realizing the level of financial success you've attained.

FOUR GROUPS

The reason it's important to acknowledge your level of wealth is this: Just as all types of investors aren't created equal, neither are all investment, wealth management, and capital preservation strategies. Some strategies that are appropriate for lower-net-worth investors are not a good fit for people with $10 million or $20 million in assets, and some of the most powerful wealth preservation tools are available only to people who have several million to invest.

If you think like a middle-class investor, you will act like one. That means you might never benefit from some of the most effective tools in the financial advisor's arsenal—tools that could increase your returns, reduce your risk, and help you pass more wealth on to your children and grandchildren.

Which wealth class are you in? That depends on your net worth. Here's a simple guide that provides a rough breakdown:

Level	Net Worth
Affluent	$250,000–$1 million
Middle-Class Millionaire	$1 million–$5 million
High Net Worth	$5 million–$25 million
Ultra-High Net Worth	> $25 million

If you have $500,000 in a 401(k) account, you are doing pretty well and likely want to do better. You are what I call *Affluent*. You pay attention to the markets, and it's a 50/50 bet that you don't have a financial advisor working for you. (That's a bad idea, but I'll get to that later.) You're probably getting a lot of your financial advice from *Money* magazine, *Kiplinger's*, "The Dave Ramsey Show," and similar sources. Your focus is 100 percent on being able to retire comfortably, so returns are your primary focus. You need consistent performance so you can participate in as much of the market's upside as possible.

If you have $3 million in assets, you're what I call a *Middle-Class Millionaire*, or MCM. You're prosperous, but you live a relatively simple, upper-middle-class lifestyle, with a nice house that's not pretentious, maybe a boat, perhaps a couple of rental properties. You're more likely to have a financial advisor, but your main focus is still rate of return, with risk management a close second.

However, if you are a higher-net-worth investor with a net worth of $5 million to $25 million (what I call *High Net Worth*, or HNW) or more than $25 million (*Ultra-High Net Worth*, or UHNW), your goals are (or should be) different. Your sources of investing information should be different too. There's nothing wrong with the advice you get from reading David Bach or listening to Suze Orman, but it's one-size-fits-all advice: Invest in index funds, max out your tax-advantaged retirement accounts, build an emergency fund of cash . . . that sort of thing. For those in the Affluent category, that advice can certainly be beneficial.

However, if you are a Middle-Class Millionaire or enjoy even higher net worth, you need personalized financial strategies that include strategies for tax planning, estate planning, charitable giving, and beyond. After all, the average household income of a *Kiplinger's* reader is about $267,000[3] while the median household income of a *Fortune* subscriber is $97,833.[4] But $2 million in assets brings with it a whole new world of opportunities and challenges. When you have $2 million, $10 million, or $20 million in assets, your challenges become greater and your needs become more complex, so you need a more sophisticated approach than the average person with $500,000 in a 401(k) account. You need *comprehensive wealth management.*

WHICH CLASS ARE YOU IN?

You might not be sure which wealth class you fall into. That's not uncommon; when you're leading a busy life, it's easy to lose track of what you have accumulated. So before we go any further, complete this simple quiz to discover to which group you belong.

When you subtract your total liabilities from your total assets, the result is your approximate net worth. Now, based on the guide provided earlier (page 6), you can easily determine your category.

If you're Affluent, don't put the book down; if you aspire to greater wealth in the future, you can definitely learn a lot from the wealth maximization strategies used by higher-net-worth investors. You might even get an important head start on implementing some of them. Let's face it, the sooner you start, the greater your opportunity for success.

If you're a Middle-Class Millionaire, you may have realized that you've outgrown most of the cookie-cutter advice provided by various media sources. However, you're not in the higher-net-worth classes yet. This book is ideal for you, because it's your

Wealth Class Quiz

Your net worth equals your assets minus your liabilities. Fill in the blanks as accurately as you can, and then total it up. That's your approximate net worth.

ASSETS

Current value of your home: _____

Current value of other real estate you own: _____

Current value of vehicles you own: _____

Current value of any retirement accounts
such as IRAs, 401(k)s, etc.: _____

Current value of other investments not part of your retirement
accounts (individual stocks, bonds, mutual funds, etc.): _____

Current value of your business as determined by
a professional valuation: _____

Cash value of any life insurance you own: _____

Total balance of checking and savings accounts: _____

Current value of any collectibles: _____

Total of all assets: _____

LIABILITIES

Total balance of the principal on all your mortgages: _____

Total balance owed on any auto or vehicle loans: _____

Total balance of any outstanding student loans: _____

Total balance owed on any other loans,
including business loans: _____

Total credit card balances: _____

Total of all liabilities: _____

Subtract liabilities from assets: _____

guide to crossing what I call the "wealth line" into that kind of extraordinary wealth. While some of the estate planning strategies discussed herein may not apply to you, many of the ideas and methods will be perfectly suited to your situation. Pay special attention to the "Crossing the Wealth Line" section at the end of each chapter. These sections will provide you with practical advice on how you can reach High Net Worth status.

If you're High Net Worth or Ultra-High Net Worth, then reading this book is a *must*. I've been working with HNW and UHNW individuals for more than 15 years, and I know what sets you apart from other investors:

» While MCMs might have most of their assets in a tax-advantaged IRA or 401(k), you probably have a lot of yours tied up in a business and/or in taxable (nonqualified) accounts.

» Because of this, your priorities are tax minimization, reducing volatility, transferring assets to your children, funding your favorite charities, and sleeping well at night.

» While you're interested in returns, you're more interested in avoiding strikeouts than hitting home runs. Now that you've accumulated your wealth, you want stability, a smooth ride, steady returns, and less stress. You understand that the market is a roller coaster, but you would rather ride the kiddie coaster.

» You met your retirement goals years ago, so you don't need autopilot target date funds or robo-advisors. You need custom-tailored investment and wealth management strategies designed to help you craft your family's future.

Sound about right? Even if none of these descriptions matches you perfectly, the message is clear: You're beyond Finance 101. Modern financial markets and wealth management tools are too complex and sophisticated for a cookie-cutter approach. Your situation is unique and requires a different approach—and different professional advice—from that which applies for people with less to invest.

THE SOONER, THE BETTER

I've written this book to be a clear, no-nonsense resource, and reading it should be like sitting across the table from a financial expert for an informative chat. My goal is to give you a clear explanation of the broad array of strategies available to the higher-net-worth investor, some of which you may never have even heard of. Will you graduate with a PhD in wealth management when you finish reading it? No. But this book will inspire you to seek out the professional help necessary to implement the strategies discussed. You can take it to your financial advisor and ask, "See what Mark talks about on page 112? Can you do this for me?"

If you're not working with a high-caliber professional advisory team, this book is also a wake-up call. You cannot go it alone in this complicated and ever-changing environment. The strategies I'm going to tell you about are not DIY. They require the extensive knowledge and steady hand of an experienced wealth manager, advisory team, or firm with the resources and training you need in order to maximize your financial success.

If you work with an advisor already, good for you. But it's time to consider this: Is the person who helped you go from zero to $2 million the right person to take you to $20 million? Have you outgrown your current advisor? This book will help you figure that out. Most important of all, it will jump-start your next-level financial plan sooner, not later. If you aspire to financial independence, peace of mind, and a brighter future for yourself, your family, and the causes you support, there's no time to waste. The sooner you implement the strategies contained in these pages, the better.

Each of the following chapters offers a key to unlocking the secrets of extraordinary wealth. In revealing these keys, we will also look at common myths that a lot of higher-net-worth individuals hold on to, and then shatter them with a dose of reality and hard facts. These myths are dangerous; they keep a lot of wealthy people from becoming even wealthier, and they also prevent the Affluent from accumulating the kind of wealth they need to reach their most cherished goals. We're going to replace them with knowledge, solid financial principles, and insights from the experience of my peers and colleagues, and from my own experience working with high-net-worth clients. Consider this a graduate-level wealth management class!

Now, whether you merely aspire to be wealthy or you have already reached your wealth goals and simply want to preserve more of what you've spent a lifetime building, let's start reading. Wherever you are in your journey, you'll find something worthwhile.

I wish you all the success in life.

Mark M. Tepper, CFP®

YOU'VE OUTGROWN COOKIE-CUTTER STRATEGIES

It's easy to allow yourself to slip into automatic mode when it comes to your wealth. You might buy a hot stock or pick a high-performing mutual fund here and there, but you're probably a bit hesitant to mess with your portfolio too much. After all, if it's not broken, why fix it? Even experienced amateur investors worry that the wrong move could hinder portfolio growth or generate a surprise tax bill.

The trouble is, apprehension leads to complacency, and a smart investor is never complacent. While it may be tempting to follow the same strategies that got you to the point of having investable assets worth a few million dollars or more, being comfortable with those strategies doesn't mean they represent the best path forward for you. After all, one of the reasons you're comfortable with your current selection of investments is probably that you're hearing and reading about them all the time in the mainstream media.

Mainstream media outlets like Fox Business, *Fortune*, and the like provide an abundance of financial information to receptive consumers. Unfortunately, this profusion of information has two drawbacks. First, much of it is conflicting. For example, a TV program might go on for 30 minutes about how you must own municipal bonds. But as soon as that program ends and you surf over to The Motley Fool, an article on that website insists that bonds are a terrible idea and you should really own dividend-paying stocks. One magazine tells you you're foolish not to buy a house now that interest rates are so low, while another warns you never to take on a mortgage again because bubbles are so common. It's enough to make even an experienced investor's head spin.

The second drawback of all this information is that it does not necessarily apply to you. The major financial media properties like *Kiplinger's* say in their own media kits that they target consumers with less than $1 million in investments. The reason is easy to understand: That's a broader audience, and they want to sell lots of advertising. As a result, the content they publish is written for a demographic with a different set of financial issues. Furthermore, the content of their articles is often diluted to appeal to the widest possible readership, so how can it really help you in your individual situation? If you have $2 million in assets, an article about whether to put your $5,000 in a traditional or a Roth IRA isn't going to be of much interest to you. At the same time, subjects of genuine interest to wealthy individuals, such as tax loss harvesting, receive no coverage at all.

As you approach and reach the high-net-worth stratosphere, you should be getting your financial insights from a better source: a high-caliber, professional team that specializes in the needs of people like you. Because what got you to $1 million is not going to get you to $5 million. And what got you to $5 million certainly isn't going to get you to $25 million.

BEWARE OF GENERIC EXPERTS

There are many dangers in paying too much attention to the so-called financial experts of popular culture. First, because they are primarily media brands, they don't always have the strong professional credentials you need from a financial advisor. Second, their main interest is usually their radio show or speaking tour, so they may not be current on financial news, trends, and research. Third, because they're mass market entertainers, their advice tends to be for the masses, not for the small minority of people building real wealth.

Consider the popular financial radio host, author, and speaker Dave Ramsey. In his book *Financial Peace Revisited*, Ramsey shares that while his career was booming and he was earning $250,000 a year, he was burying himself and his wife in debt in order to build his real estate portfolio. On his website he writes, "The short version of the story is that debt caused us, over the course of two and a half years of fighting it, to lose everything. We didn't tell anyone what was going on, but if we had to do it again, we would learn from the wisdom of others who have been through it."

Ramsey has said that when things began to fall apart, he took out $1.2 million in short-term loans to buy property. But when one of his major creditors sold to a larger bank, bank officials began scrutinizing his borrowing and wound up demanding that he repay his notes within 90 days. That left bankruptcy as the only option.[1]

To his credit, Ramsey has been transparent about his bankruptcy and has used his own horror story to educate others on the perils of debt and getting in over your head. His life experiences are probably valuable to people who might be buried in debt and on the precipice of bankruptcy. If you're not in that situation, however, you're probably better off learning and taking guidance from professionals who have experiences working with people like you—whether you classify yourself as a business owner, an executive, a professional, or a higher-net-worth investor.

A NEW ATTITUDE TOWARD WEALTH

Believing yourself to be wealthy, by the way, is not elitism. It's realism. But some Americans shy away from thinking of themselves as wealthy, because they believe including themselves in that category will make them seem arrogant or elitist. In his book *Coming Apart*, Charles Murray observes that since the founding of the country, Americans have stubbornly refused to talk about themselves in terms of class distinctions like rich and poor. That refusal persists today.

To many people, calling someone "wealthy" is an insult. We live in an era of Occupy protests and anger at the "1 percent." Even though a 2005 paper published by the National Bureau of Economic Research[2] found that higher-educated, higher-earning Americans work more hours than people in lower-income groups, there persists this idea that being working class is inherently virtuous while there's something unseemly or immoral about being wealthy.

Not true. As best-selling author Rory Vaden writes on his website, "We can have money without having it be the place [from which] we derive our self-worth. We can make money without making it what defines us." He continues:

> There are plenty of rich people who are good people, and there are plenty of rich people who are jerks. Just like there are plenty of poor people who are good people and there are plenty of poor people who are jerks. Having money doesn't make you good or bad, right or wrong, successful or unsuccessful. Having money just means that you have money. Not having money just means that you don't have money. And losing our emotional attachment to money frees us up to have power over it, to use it and earn it more effectively.

The fact is, the wealthy contribute a great deal to society. According to the Almanac of American Philanthropy, the top 1 percent in net worth make one-third of the country's total charitable donations.[3] Wealthy individuals also give back by starting nonprofit foundations, some of which—like the Bill & Melinda Gates Foundation and the Ford Foundation—make major contributions in everything from medical research and early childhood education to the fine arts. Companies started by wealthy people create jobs and encourage innovations that keep America's economy growing. Bottom line: Accumulating substantial wealth (and using it responsibly) is nothing to be ashamed of. It's something to be proud of.

Despite this, unhealthy thinking about money may have crept into your mind and kept you from acknowledging where you reside on the wealth ladder. If it has, it's in your best interest to acknowledge your reservations and then let them go, because they're holding you back from taking steps that will ensure your financial well-being—and that of your children.

Most of the people who fall into the higher-net-worth groups did not inherit their money; they earned their wealth through years and years of hard work and sacrifice. If you belong to the higher-net-worth groups, there is a strong possibility that you accumulated your wealth by starting a business. According to the Internal Revenue Service, more than 72 percent of Americans who earn more than $1 million per year own part or all of a partnership or S corporation.[4] If you look at Americans who earn $10 million a year or more, that number rises to 90 percent.

There are other paths to prosperity, of course. Most of the wealthy who didn't start businesses accumulated their wealth by working as corporate executives or by becoming professionals in such fields as law and medicine. But what matters is that after you started your business or began in your profession, you put in years of relentless hard work. Whether you started a small manufacturing company or launched your own law firm, you put in long hours and invested blood, sweat, and tears to make your business successful. If you had to climb the corporate ladder, the same rule applies: Work equals wealth. You've sacrificed in other areas of life to get to where you are now. You've earned everything you have today. This is your victory lap, and implementing a wealth management strategy that's appropriate for the complexity of your situation will make that lap long and satisfying.

YOUR NEEDS ARE DIFFERENT

The investment and financial planning concerns of the Affluent and the Middle-Class Millionaire are not the same as those of people with a higher net worth. Therefore, the financial planning and investments strategies that are most beneficial to each group are quite different. Let's take a look at some of the features and needs that are common among individuals who are High Net Worth and Ultra-High Net Worth.

If you have accumulated assets of $5 million or more, you're probably financially independent or well on your way to being so.

You might already be retired, but if you're not, retirement is not an issue. Your number one goal is protecting capital against taxes, litigation, and volatility.

Is that about right? Let's consider some other things that differentiate you.

» **You need investment planning.** Most of the people in the $100,000–to–$1 million group will have most of their money in tax-deferred vehicles. But somebody who has $7.5 million in assets will hold much of it in a taxable environment by default. If that's you, your strategy has to be different. Your objectives are not absolute returns, but after-tax wealth creation and volatility reduction. This requires a more complex set of investment choices, from individual securities to alternative asset strategies. Building and balancing your portfolio is an art form that requires skill and extensive knowledge.

» **You need tax planning.** An Affluent family with $250,000 in assets that's in the 28 percent federal tax bracket doesn't need elaborate tax planning; they need H&R Block. But if your family is in the 39.6 percent federal bracket, you need strategies that will minimize your tax obligation. Say you're bringing home a $500,000 annual income, which doesn't have to be salary—if you own a business, some of that income could be from profits. Between state, federal, and local taxes, you could be giving 50 percent of your income to the government. Tax planning is a critical facet of your wealth management picture. The more you make, the more important tax planning becomes.

» **You need estate planning.** Despite political rhetoric, the so-called death tax isn't going anywhere. But it doesn't affect Affluent or MCM investors, so they don't have to think about it. The way the estate tax is currently structured, a married couple gets a free pass on roughly the first $11 million of their estate. They can pass that much to their beneficiaries tax-free. Above that, they are taxed at 40 percent, plus (possibly) state tax. That's not an issue for people with fewer assets; they don't have $11 million to pass on. But if you have a great deal of wealth, especially in the form of a business, now is the time to start implementing aggressive strategies to keep that wealth in the family without passing on an undue burden to your heirs. After all, Uncle Sam isn't your real uncle.

» **You're not into the hot stock of the day.** You hold a lot of low-turnover investments such as index funds, exchange-traded funds (ETFs), or individual stocks and bonds. You know that turnover inside a mutual fund can trigger a taxable event, so you avoid it. When it comes to stocks, you steer toward the kinds of stable companies that Warren Buffett owns: well-known companies that will continue to run profitable businesses for decades. None of your holdings are glamorous; the only glamorous thing is the consistent growth of your wealth over time.

» **Retirement is the last thing on your mind (and rightfully so).** Lower-income investors tend to have retirement tunnel vision, so they need a financial plan that's all about retirement. You have bigger goals and objectives and can afford to see the bigger picture. You know that as you increase in wealth, financial planning increases in complexity. Your goals have to do with your lifestyle and legacy. You want to protect your wealth from taxes, losses, and lawsuits, and also support the causes you care about. You don't want to monitor your portfolio personally, but nor do you want to be blindsided by a market correction. You are interested in ongoing *strategic financial planning,* not a one-time plan that gives you the green light to retire.

» **You're interested in options not available to lower-net-worth groups.** Affluents and Middle-Class Millionaires might use alternative assets such as real estate, but otherwise they're probably going to have most of their assets in a mix of traditional funds that own stocks and bonds. Because you have more assets to invest, you have a world of other instruments available to you. Many of these strategies are historically accessed via private investment (although we are seeing the evolution of public options) and carry their own risks. However, the general purpose of these strategies is to either enhance overall returns or, more important, reduce your overall portfolio risk.

» **Risk reduction is achieved by adding strategies that offer a return stream not correlated to traditional stocks and bonds.** You might invest in private equity, making capital available to private companies that want to develop new products, expand, or acquire other businesses. You might buy commercial real estate, taking advantage of strong economic growth and long lease terms to create cash flow while acquiring assets that increase in value. You might get into hedge funds or private limited partnerships that use the collective funds from multiple investors to generate returns using a variety of strategies. You could get into venture capital, providing funds for startup businesses that offer substantial growth potential. As someone in a high-net-worth group, you can consider a combination of these investment strategies to lower the risk to your portfolio.

» **You'd like to direct the timing of capital gains and losses.** If you're in one of the lower-net-worth groups, you might deal with capital gains tax issues when you sell a piece of real estate, but otherwise their impact is minimal. However, in the higher-net-worth world, capital gains can potentially generate significant tax bills. Strategic tools are available to reduce your tax obligation, but it's not quite that simple; depending on your blend of short- and long-term gains and losses, your tax planning can become very complicated. Hence the need for a comprehensive, end-to-end financial solution.

PLAN USING A DIFFERENT PLAYBOOK

Different needs, different ambitions, different levels of wealth—with all these at play, you definitely need a different playbook, because you are not subject to the same rules as people with fewer investable assets. There are opportunities available to you simply because the minimum dollar amount needed to invest in certain asset classes is too high for lower-net-worth individuals. Now is the time to start approaching your wealth management from a different perspective, because the sooner you begin implementing strategies targeted at higher-net-worth individuals, the sooner you will start seeing real benefits from them.

I would also suggest doing the following:

» **Clean up your media diet.** If your household makes $125,000 a year, you're fine consuming *Kiplinger's* and *Money*. If you're a higher-net-worth individual, however, you should not be getting your investment advice from the mass media. Remember, these articles, blog posts, and television and radio shows are providing cookie-cutter advice designed for people with one goal in mind: retirement. That isn't you; your goals are more complex. Get your financial information from a team of trained professionals who know how to interpret complicated data and turn that data into actionable investing intelligence. It's fine to read the financial publications or websites, but do it for fun and out of interest, not because you're looking for advice on which stocks to buy.

» **Review and reset your goals.** If you have been thinking of yourself as a Middle-Class Millionaire for years, you may still be stuck on retirement as your main goal. However, if you have climbed into the higher-net-worth groups, it's time to move beyond retirement to more far-reaching goals. Some of these are basic and apply to everyone: You want to avoid paying a single dollar of federal, state, or local income tax that you don't have to. You want a portfolio of investments that are stable, with low turnover so you're not subject to taxable events that stick you with an unexpected tax bill.

» **Beyond that, things get more personal.** Do you want to pass a business down to your children? Invest in young entrepreneurs? Protect your family against your untimely demise? Give to charities that you care about? Start your own non-profit foundation and provide scholarships? Get a building at your alma mater named for you? Or just travel the world and not have to worry about your investments for the rest of your life, ever? There are ways to accomplish all of your goals, but not until you know what they are. If you're not sure, the time to begin thinking about these things is now.

» **End your DIY wealth management.** In most areas, people who insist on the do-it-yourself approach wind up losing a lot more than they save. Sure, hiring a licensed contractor to replace your old windows might cost you $15,000. However, if you do the same work yourself, with no experience, you're likely to make lots of mistakes, have leaks that damage your home, and wind up hiring a contractor anyway—not just to replace the windows but to repair the damage you caused. Final cost: $25,000. There's a saying for that: *Penny wise and pound foolish.*

But that's relatively low-stakes stuff. You wouldn't diagnose your own heart disease or defend yourself against a criminal charge in court, right? Of course not. And when you get to $10 million net worth, you should not be managing your own finances, either. The markets, the financial instruments, and the web of laws and regulations are dizzyingly complex. It takes a team of people with professional certifications and years of hands-on experience to design your comprehensive plan, execute it every day, and adapt it in response to changing markets and your changing life.

If you love investing, trading, and learning about finance too much to go cold turkey, there's a simple solution. Take a small amount—say, $100,000—and open an account at a discount online brokerage like Schwab. Use that as your DIY "mad money" account. Buy and sell stocks, mess with asset allocation, and enjoy being hands-on with your money, all without risking your entire financial well-being. If you get a strong return, that's a bonus.

» **Stop listening to the wrong people.** Money is a subject that fascinates just about everyone, so everybody seems to have advice on which stocks to buy, when to sell, and how to invest. But consider the source. It's one thing to listen to Uncle Nick or your dental hygienist when you're considering where to shop for a mortgage; it's another matter when you're talking about investing decisions that will shape the next few decades of your life. When you reach High Net Worth or Ultra-High Net Worth status, the stakes change. Tune out the noise and listen to professionals.

That doesn't just mean tuning out well-meaning relatives and friends with hot stock tips; it also means taking the advice of your financial professionals only when they are talking about their specific area of professional expertise. Your CPA may be brilliant, but he's a specialist in accounting, not wealth management. Pay close attention when your attorney talks to you about tax law or incorporation, but don't treat her thoughts on ETFs or risk-adjusted returns as anything more than friendly suggestions. When the questions relate to your investment strategy, portfolio management, or long-term goals, there's only one person you should be listening to: a well-credentialed, professional financial advisor.

» **Change your attitude toward returns.** Warren Buffett once said that owning stocks should be like watching paint dry: dull but with a desirable result. That's the attitude you should become comfortable with. Lower-income investors need to ride the market roller coaster because they need a big payoff in order to meet their retirement goals, especially if they waited too long to start saving. You don't need home runs, so stop swinging so hard. Choke up on the bat. Focus on avoiding strikeouts. Financial thrill seeking can be fun when you're younger, but later in life your finances should offer a smooth, relatively predictable ride. That way, you're free to seek your thrills in other ways, whether that means traveling the world or trying a new life pursuit.

When you've achieved a higher net worth, investing stops being all about returns and starts being about a long-term, comprehensive vision for your *entire* life. Stop thinking exclusively about your rate of return. Start thinking about how much wealth you keep after taxes, how you're maximizing the saleable value of your business, how you can pass on wealth to your heirs without also passing on a tax burden, and how you can guard against litigation losses with smart strategies you've probably never heard of. This is the time of life when you want to preserve, grow, and enjoy.

Crossing the Wealth Line

» *Tune out the noise. Watch CNBC and Fox Business for financial news—not stock tips. In any given day, you may come across one analyst who loves a stock and another who despises the same stock.*

» *Tune out your friends. They're not professional money managers. Keep in mind that whenever your buddies tell you about their hot stock pick, they've got other stocks that are strikeouts that they're not sharing with you. People love to brag about their winners, but they rarely mention their losers.*

» *Don't micromanage your financial advisor. Find someone you're comfortable with, and let them do their job. They don't tell you how to do your job, whether it's making widgets or performing heart surgery, so don't tell them how to do theirs.*

WEALTH MANAGEMENT IS SO MUCH MORE THAN INVESTING

When thinking about your finances means thinking mostly about saving for retirement, it makes sense to think in terms of investment management. After all, your main goal is to invest for the highest possible return. Even when you're putting money into a 529 account for your child's college education, you're still focused on investing and returns. There are other aspects to your financial life—insurance, real estate, taxes—but you either handle those yourself or hire a tax preparer, accountant, or real estate agent as the need arises.

When people in the Affluent or MCM groups do hire a financial advisor, that person is usually managing investments—various securities (stocks, bonds, etc.) and other assets (e.g., real estate)— in order to meet specified goals. That's important work, but its objective is to maximize returns, file required tax paperwork, and not much else. As we have discussed, that might be fine for someone with $500,000 in investable assets, but for someone with $10 million for whom retirement is a *fait accompli*, investment management is just not sufficient.

Look at it this way: Your level of wealth usually correlates with the complexity of what you had to do to build that wealth. If you're in the Affluent class with $500,000 in assets, it's likely that you accumulated those assets by working hard, saving in a tax-advantaged retirement account, buying your home, and maybe purchasing a rental property when you could scrape together the down payment. Your financial life is relatively simple. You still need smart investment management, basic estate planning documents, and sound tax preparation. With those services, reaching your goals becomes possible.

Unless you inherit it, you don't accumulate $10 million of investable assets without sacrifice. You do it through actions that by their very nature make your finances more complicated, such as starting and growing a business, studying hard through medical school, or working your way up the corporate ladder. That level of wealth also tends to bring additional challenges. You pay the highest marginal tax rate and are a prime target for future federal tax rate increases. You're also more likely to be audited. According to figures from 2014, the IRS audited 16.22 percent of taxpayers with incomes over $10 million, compared to 0.5 percent of people with incomes between $75,000 and $100,000. And according to the 2016 U.S. Trust® Study of High Net Worth Philanthropy, there's a 91 percent chance that you gave to charity last year, and the odds are also good that some of your assets will be subject to the federal estate tax.

In other words, your finances are much more complex than buying and selling a few stocks and receiving 1099 forms in the mail. You need more than basic investment consulting. Complex financial situations require sophisticated solutions. That solution is *wealth management.*

WHAT IS WEALTH MANAGEMENT?

You already know what investment consulting is. It's what 99 percent of smaller investors—and some large ones—think financial advisors are supposed to spend all their time doing: picking stocks, buying and selling funds, and so on. And with many firms, that's true. A survey of financial advisory firms nationwide conducted by CEG Worldwide determined that 93.4 percent of firms are investment generalists, while only 6.6 percent provide comprehensive wealth management services to their clients. While many firms claim to be "wealth managers," very few provide true wealth management.

True wealth management combines investment consulting, financial planning, accounting and tax services, estate planning, and legal services into a single comprehensive package. So wealth management includes investment consulting and asset management, but then goes far beyond it to include what is collectively known as *advanced planning*:

» *Wealth enhancement*, centered on cash flow enhancement and tax minimization strategies

» *Wealth transfer*, centered on sound estate planning

» *Wealth protection*, centered on safeguarding assets from creditors and legal judgments

» *Charitable giving*, centered on maximizing the impact of philanthropic efforts

Another significant piece of wealth management is *relationship management*, in which your financial advisor coordinates the activities of your team of financial professionals, including your accountant, your attorney, and your insurance professional.

So, sound wealth management can be defined accordingly:

Wealth management = investment consulting +
advanced planning + relationship management

However, wealth management can (and often does) go beyond these categories to encompass everything related to your long-term prosperity. For example, a wealth manager might also assist clients in purchasing liability insurance, managing a family trust, or helping implement strategies to enhance the value of a closely held business.

Is comprehensive wealth management the right answer for

you and your financial goals? To help you decide, let's take a closer look at each component of advanced planning.

WEALTH ENHANCEMENT

Wealth enhancement refers mainly to two areas: *cash flow maximization* and *tax minimization*, which basically mean that your financial team is making sure you have as much as possible coming in while keeping as little as possible going out to Uncle Sam. If you own a business, you're already familiar with the concept of cash flow. It's your lifeblood, and one of the ways you've grown your business is by taking that "free" cash flow—the money that remains after you have met all your expenses—and investing it in growing your company. Do that wisely and repeatedly, and you'll be quite successful.

Your wealth manager should be helping you apply the same principle to your personal cash flow. *Cash flow maximization* is about optimizing the funds you have available from your personal income stream so that you can do more to grow your wealth. There are several ways to do this:

» **Reduce the amount you pay in taxes.** Tax minimization, which is discussed in a few pages, allows you to invest the savings to increase your wealth. There are many strategies that can help you accomplish this, but if your investment consultant doesn't know about them, you can't benefit from them.

» **Trim wasteful spending from your lifestyle.** This does not mean you have to deprive yourself or curtail activities or luxuries that you enjoy. However, wealthy people are busy people, and busy people often say yes to an expense without looking at lower-cost alternatives. A thorough audit of your personal expenses usually reveals many ways you can trim costs without impacting your lifestyle at all. For example, do you lease your cars? Maybe you shouldn't. According to research by author Thomas Corley,[1] only 6 percent of the wealthy lease their cars, because leasing comes with a much higher total cost of ownership than buying. You're much better off buying a quality car and keeping it for years. It's not hard to imagine how a list of simple changes to your spending and budgeting habits can leave more cash in your pocket.

» **Use debt wisely to produce savings.** Good debt is debt whose interest is tax deductible, such as your home mortgage, which is backed by an investment (your house); bad debt has nondeductible interest and includes credit cards and car loans that fund consumption. Debt is generally something to minimize and pay down when possible, but there are ways to make it work to your advantage. Let's say you're in the market for a vacation home and you've identified a condo that you can purchase for $500,000. While you may have the funds available to pay cash, don't pull the trigger too quickly. If those funds are invested in a balanced portfolio with an expected return of 5 percent annually, and a 30-year mortgage on the house would cost you 4 percent, you're better off financing the purchase. The positive interest rate arbitrage of 1 percent (5 percent minus 4 percent) will have your portfolio ahead by $173,924 over the course of those 30 years. How much work did you put into realizing that extra wealth? Not much. That's a no-brainer.

Tax minimization reflects a simple desire that we all have: to give Uncle Sam as little as possible of our hard-earned money while still complying with the law. This begins with simple steps such as your accounting and tax team documenting every expense and knowing the tax laws so you can claim every possible deduction. After that, there are a number of tried-and-true strategies.

You could open a high-limit qualified retirement account like a defined benefit pension plan, with a contribution limit of $215,000 in 2017 (no, that's not a typo), and then contribute the maximum. You could take accelerated depreciation on most tangible and some intangible assets to deduct the cost of wear and tear or obsolescence. You could take every possible business deduction to reduce your taxable personal income. You could deduct the cost of some types of insurance. You could donate stock to qualified charities and get an adjustment if the stock has appreciated since you purchased it. You could design your investment portfolio so that the majority of your income is tax-exempt or comes through capital gains and qualified dividends, which are taxed at a lower rate than personal income.

The list goes on, and there's no need to get into detail on all the possibilities here. Suffice it to say, for the higher-net-worth individual, especially one who owns a business, there are numerous ways to legally reduce tax obligations. Doing so is a cornerstone of sound wealth management.

WEALTH TRANSFER

Wealth transfer is simply about figuring out how to transfer as much of your wealth as possible to your beneficiaries while minimizing the tax burden that you also transfer to them. As you may have heard (because it's been hyped by every media outlet on the planet for the past 10 years), we're just beginning the largest transfer of wealth in history as the aging baby boomers begin gifting more than $30 trillion to their children, grandchildren, and favorite charities. But that doesn't have to mean headaches for you or tax bills for your beneficiaries.

You may know that if your estate equals less than approximately $5.5 million ($11 million for a couple), it's not subject to the federal estate tax. But did you know that states also have their own estate taxes with varying exemptions, ranging from high exemption limits like Delaware's to surprisingly low limits in New Jersey? So even if you have a smaller estate, don't assume you will see no benefit from a smart wealth transfer plan.

Wealth transfer begins with lifetime gifts: amounts up to $14,000 per year that you can give to beneficiaries free of gift or estate taxes. It moves on to a dizzying range of trusts, charitable gifts, and other instruments that require considerable expertise to set up and manage. There are also specific strategies you can use to pass a business to your heirs without burdening them with an onerous tax debt. Creating a limited liability company (LLC) or a family limited partnership (FLP) can also be useful in wealth transfer.

Tight coordination and careful review between your accountant and tax attorney can make such wealth transfer measures rock solid and can deliver benefits not only to you but also to future generations.

WEALTH PROTECTION

Apart from taxation and inflation, the primary threat to the assets of higher-net-worth Americans is unjust seizure by creditors through legal action. The harsh reality of our legal system is that if you have deep pockets, you are a potential target, regardless of whether the lawsuit is justified. You're also a potential target if you come into a windfall through an inheritance, the sale of a business, or some other means. Part of your wealth management team's job is to take proactive steps to protect your assets from legal threats.

This could include the commonsense step of increasing your liability insurance coverage. An umbrella liability policy, which covers a broad range of potential liability situations, is comparatively inexpensive. Yet according to Trusted Choice, an association of independent insurance agents and brokers, one in five wealthy individuals have no umbrella coverage. An umbrella liability policy that covers an amount *at least* equal to your total net worth, if not more, is prudent for individuals with a high net worth. The insurance expert on your wealth management team will give you specifics, but in general, umbrella liability coverage is very inexpensive, with $2 million in protection typically costing $300 to $400 a year.

Your wealth management team will develop a complete strategic plan for wealth protection, including keeping a percentage of your personal assets separate and secure in case of divorce, protecting yourself from business liability by turning a sole proprietorship into an LLC or a corporation, shielding wealth from the possible actions of business partners, and many other options. If you happen to be in a profession with a high risk of malpractice litigation, such as medicine or law, your team will recommend insurance solutions in those areas as well.

CHARITABLE GIVING

Many financial advisors encounter clients who are active in charitable giving. For these investors, it's imperative to maximize the impact of their charitable contributions—not just for the charities, but also for them! For higher-net-worth individuals, charitable giving should be more than simply scratching a check; it can be part of a tax minimization strategy that also supports important causes. Solutions can include donor-advised funds, family foundations, charitable remainder trusts, and more. The key is to identify the optimal strategies for accomplishing your goals and the goals of each charity.

RELATIONSHIP MANAGEMENT

The final component in wealth management involves two disciplines: *client relationship management* and *professional network relationship management*. The first is self-explanatory. The financial advisor's job is to manage communication and consultation with you, the investor. That means making sure you are receiving regular updates and statements, regular phone calls or in-person meetings are occurring, and your questions are being answered quickly and thoroughly.

An effective client relationship manager will anticipate your questions before they become concerns and will recommend solutions before situations turn into problems. You should never feel uncertain or uninformed about what's happening with your portfolio, your planning, or your financial picture.

The other part of relationship management—managing the professional network—might seem less important, but it's critical. You need a single responsible individual (usually your financial advisor) coordinating the efforts of all the other professionals on your financial team: tax attorneys, CPAs, insurance professionals, and anyone else whose services you need. They should all be working together toward the same goals, and you should not be the intermediary between them. Your advisor should quarterback the coordination.

Coordination and cooperation aren't the only reason this service matters. You also need your advisor to remind each professional to provide advice only in his or her field of expertise. It's quite common for people working within an integrated financial team to offer advice that contradicts sound financial practice or even harms the client's interests. For example, on numerous occasions CPAs, with the best of intentions, have recommended tax strategies to clients that would save on their tax bill in the current year. What those CPAs didn't consider was that their strategy would increase the client's tax bill in coming years, wiping out any immediate savings.

The financial advisor who's quarterbacking the entire wealth management team can run all ideas and recommendations through his or her office and filter out those that might be problematic. For instance, your advisor might recommend a tax strategy that costs you more today but saves you and your beneficiaries down the line. The same applies to legal advice, insurance, and charitable giving.

THE ROLE OF THE WEALTH MANAGER

True wealth managers are far more than "stock jockeys," and they do a lot more for their clients than manage their investments. For some clients, the relationship is intimate and highly personal.

While that doesn't mean you can expect your wealth manager to pick up your pizza and your dry cleaning, the reality is that many wealthy clients often come to depend on their wealth managers to be resourceful, all-purpose "fixers" for areas of their busy lives that are not (at first glance) about money.

One example that is amusing, but that also illustrates how heavily some people lean on their wealth managers, comes from writer Brooke Harrington in *Forbes*. She writes about a Hong Kong wealth manager who was asked by a client to fulfill a rather unusual request:

> I was phoned up from Osaka once by a client who said, "I'm sitting across from Owagi-san, who speaks no English, but we are bowing to each other. He has just said to me through a translator that he needs a thousand sides of smoked salmon by Tuesday, and I'm relying on you to get them." I said, "I'm your wealth manager, not your fishmonger." And the client said, "Well, today you're a fishmonger." So I had to ring up a friend who knew the guy from Unilever who runs the smoked salmon plant in Scotland. And the plant manager made it happen. So I found out later that my client was testing me by setting me an impossible task—he told me that he was trying to see if I was really up to the kind of job he wanted me to do.

You probably shouldn't expect your wealth manager to procure your seafood or make your travel arrangements for you (although many family office firms actually do these sorts of things). But when it comes to using the tools of portfolio management, accounting, tax law, and estate planning to create the secure, fulfilling life that you've worked toward all these years, a good wealth manager may be the leader, advisor, and ally you've been looking for.

WEALTH MANAGERS ADD VALUE

For some, the major objection to signing up for a comprehensive suite of wealth management services is the cost; it's not cheap to retain the services of a team of highly trained, expert professionals. Some practices may charge 1 percent of your total assets under management per year, though the more assets you bring to the table, the lower the percentage. However, all bias aside, wealth management services are worth the cost.

There's more to wealth management than the gross or net rate of return on your statement. A good wealth management firm providing advanced planning will generate additional alpha—real, measurable added value. A good advisor with a strong team can add several hundred basis points of alpha per year to your net worth by implementing sound advanced planning strategies.

What's this "alpha" thing financial advisors speak of? Alpha is a measure of risk-adjusted return—the number that indicates how much an actual return exceeds a benchmark like the S&P 500 index while taking into consideration comparable risk. One hundred basis points of alpha equals 1 percent of incremental risk-adjusted returns.

The Vanguard Group, one of the most highly respected investment management companies in the world, has calculated the value that wealth management delivers to clients. Vanguard estimates that when you take into account managing investor behavior, asset allocation and rebalancing, spending strategies, and other tactics, a strong wealth management team can add about 300 basis points of alpha, or 3 percent in risk-adjusted return, to a client's portfolio per year.[2]

Moving from the scenario described to Vanguard Advisor's Alpha methodology

Vanguard Advisor's Alpha Strategy	Module	Typical Value Added for Client (basis points)
Suitable asset allocation using broadly diversified funds/ETFs	I	>0bps*
Cost-effective implmentation (expsense ratios)	II	40 bps
Rebalancing	III	35 bps
Behavioral coaching	IV	150 bps
Asset location	V	0 to 75 bps
Spending strategy (withdrawal order)	VI	0 to 110 bps
Total-return versus income investing	VII	>0bps*
Total potential value added		About 3% in net returns

*Value is deemed significant but too unique to each investor to quantify

45

If an additional 3 percent doesn't seem like much, consider this:

» An investor with a $10 million portfolio earning 7 percent per year would have about $38.7 million in assets after 20 years, before inflation and taxation.

» The same investor with that extra 300 basis points would earn 10 percent per year. After 20 years, all else being equal, the investor would have about $67 million before inflation and taxation.

That's a simple calculation, but it shows you the impact of a sound wealth management program. That second investor would have nearly $30 million in additional pretax wealth to build a business, support a charity, pass on to various heirs, or do whatever he or she chooses. Of course, good advisors cost money. In fact, as with most things in life, you get what you pay for. When choosing a financial advisor, don't cut corners. It won't pay off in the long run.

Wealth management is also extremely valuable to the Middle-Class Millionaire. For MCMs, investing is still all about making that "number" so they can retire. Consider the difference 300 basis points could make to a $1 million portfolio over 20 years:

» At 7 percent, the investor would have about $3.9 million in assets before taxation and inflation.

» With the additional alpha taking that up to 10 percent, the investor would have $6.7 million before inflation and taxation.

That extra $2.8 million could be the difference between our MCM retiring at 52 and sailing the Caribbean for 20 years and retiring at 67, when both the MCM and his or her spouse are more likely to experience health problems that will prevent them from living the life they've dreamed about for so long. Middle-Class Millionaires can't afford to miss out on alpha-generating opportunities.

It should be clear that wealth management is much more than investment consulting. Investment consulting is an important component of wealth management, but wealth management is a big-picture approach for people who are concerned about much more than gross returns—people who are also concerned about minimizing risk, protecting capital, and enjoying a smooth ride through life.

How well are you doing in each of these areas? If you were a wealth management student, would you give yourself a grade of A+ or C- today? Before you go any further, here's the chance to complete a unique 15-minute online assessment that will identify your strengths and weaknesses as an investor. The resulting report will help you hone your focus and improve your wealth management situation. Find it at www.wealthalyze.com.

Crossing the Wealth Line

» *Even if you don't need a wealth manager right now, when you choose your financial advisory team, be sure to align yourself with professionals who are strong in more than just investments. You need a team of professionals with specific expertise in tax, estate planning, asset protection, risk management, and beyond. Over time, they can provide you with many ideas that will help grow your wealth.*

WITHOUT PROPER PLANNING, SUCCESS IS A PIPE DREAM

One of the most persistent misconceptions in the world of investing is that financial planning is all about retirement. It's true that for the average investor, the one whose main investment vehicle is a tax-advantaged account like a 401(k) with a $400,000 balance, retirement is probably the only goal that matters. That individual isn't thinking about selling a business or starting a private foundation, so the rules are simple: Build a portfolio that delivers a significant return without much regard for risk, adjust the asset allocation periodically, and then keep saving until you reach your magical number—the amount you need in order to retire.

However, we've established that when you reach the High

Net Worth or Ultra-High Net Worth level, you are no longer subject to the normal rules. Retirement-centric solutions don't make sense. If you've invested well enough that retirement is a foregone conclusion—or if you're already retired—then congratulations are in order. But that doesn't mean you no longer need financial planning.

Even if you're confident that you've accrued enough assets to enjoy a secure and comfortable retirement, there are many other aspects of a wealthy individual's financial life that require sound planning and careful management. The fact is, money has a way of disappearing if you're not watching, and it's important to have someone watching to prevent poor decisions or simple carelessness from putting a damper on your future.

Consider what often happens to professional athletes. These men and women can make tens of millions of dollars playing baseball, football, or basketball, and millions more from endorsements and commercial deals. Granted, the average career might last only about five years, but even average pro athletes who earn long-term contracts might make $100 million or more in their careers. But shockingly, many of them wind up broke. A *Sports Illustrated* story from 2009 estimated that about 60 percent of NBA players burn through all their money within *five years* of leaving the game. It's even worse for NFL players, 78 percent of whom are bankrupt or under severe financial stress within two years of retirement.[1]

Why? The reasons aren't unusual: divorce, failed post-retirement businesses, a lavish lifestyle, fraud by personal financial managers. But there's a common thread: According to the *SI* story, most pro ballers will sit down with financial advisors to talk about managing their money, but this doesn't mean that they'll listen to the advice—or that they've chosen the right advisor. Only after the fact do they realize they were undereducated and hopelessly naïve.

As a result, some men and women with their whole lives ahead of them, who should be financially independent, often wind up bankrupt, starting over with nothing. The tragedy is that if they had followed sound advice, many of the saddest tales of woe could have been prevented. The moral is this: Having wealth doesn't mean you'll *always* have wealth. Keeping it requires getting and being receptive to good advice.

FINANCIAL PLANNING VERSUS A FINANCIAL PLAN

Before moving on, let's draw a clear line between the *idea* of financial planning and the *deliverable* that is the financial plan. *Financial planning* is a process, a dynamic road map of your life's financial journey that's proactively updated as markets, your life circumstances, and your personal goals change. A *financial plan* is a single document that might outline something like a retirement strategy. Because financial planning can add significant value to the assets of higher-net-worth investors, it should not be considered optional. If you have goals, you need financial planning, period.

An increasing number of Americans agree with this. According to a survey conducted by the CFP® Board, the organization that certifies professionals who hold the CERTIFIED FINANCIAL PLANNER™ certification, consumer use of financial advisors has jumped nearly 43 percent since 2010. Back then, in the depths of the Great Recession, just 28 percent of consumers worked with an advisor; five years later, in 2015, 40 percent said they worked with one. That's an encouraging increase. Also encouraging are the data that show wealthy individuals are more likely to rely on wealth managers and financial planners than lower-income individuals are. But it still leaves millions of Americans without any source of reliable, nonpartisan financial advice.

However, if you are not one of those who takes advantage of the services of a financial advisor—or if you are less than thrilled with your current financial advisor but haven't yet made a change—it's worth taking some time to understand just what goes into true financial planning. That's how you'll really understand its value. To begin at the beginning, you'll want to absorb three of the most important analytical tools that go into legitimate financial planning: the Monte Carlo simulation, the "life happens" philosophy, and stress testing.

THE MONTE CARLO SIMULATION

The most important thing to understand about financial planning is that it's about time. Time is the one predictable element in any financial strategy, because it always passes and it always brings changes. Do you want your life in 10 years to look the same as it does today? Of course not. You want to be better off, feel happier, have more freedom, see your kids prospering, and be living some version of your ideal, whether that means relaxing in retirement or traveling to exciting places. Time brings change, and financial planning brings as much order to that change as is humanly possible. You have a vision and goals; your plan is a road map designed to get you to those goals from now until the end of your life, and then to help your beneficiaries continue on their journeys with your assistance.

Financial planning is like a GPS; it moves with you. Some financial planners treat planning as though they're working with a static map: They locate a new client on the map, draw an X, and that's it. That works—as long as the client doesn't move. But people aren't static; they have kids, change jobs, bail out their adult children, purchase second homes, and more. Life is fluid, and a lot can happen in even five years—especially when you're wealthy. You could have a business that grows or contracts, investments tied to volatile overseas markets, or any number of other challenges unique to higher-net-worth individuals. No static, one-time financial plan can remain relevant in those situations. If your plan doesn't change with you, in a few years it will become obsolete.

True financial planning is all about managing and reducing risk over time—about predicting the likelihood of trouble with the highest possible accuracy and then designing a plan that will keep you on target should the worst happen. The most proactive firms will update that plan every year to identify potential issues before they become irreversible financial mistakes.

One way to do that is by running Monte Carlo simulations: computer algorithms that calculate the effect of expected returns and volatility (known as the *standard deviation*) on your financial plan over your lifetime. Like gambling in the Monaco hot spot, these simulations involve chance and random outcomes. Investing comes with varying levels of volatility, and the higher your potential return, the higher your risk exposure. A Monte Carlo simulation runs your plan through thousands of simulated trials, exposing it to a huge range of potential return scenarios, to see whether your plan will be successful under any and all conditions.

When an advisory firm puts a financial plan together, the advisors also have to make assumptions about the rate of return. Your goal (and your advisor's goal) might be to average a 6 percent return over the next 20 years, but no financial plan is going to return exactly 6 percent each year. That's the nature of markets: They rise and fall from year to year. One year, your portfolio might be up 20 percent and you're feeling like a king; the next, you might be down 10 perfect and you're ready to sell the summer house. A Monte Carlo simulation considers these ups and downs by looking at the standard deviation in each asset class where you're invested and randomizing returns to account for that deviation. Instead of looking at what your portfolio will do at a steady 6 percent per year, the computer randomizes all the possible rates of return and determines how often your portfolio will hit your required number.

The result is a percentage value: the chance that with your current plan, you will have money left in your portfolio if you live the number of years you're expected to live. Most advisors consider 70 percent or higher to represent a solid financial strategy. If your simulation scored a 70, that would mean that, given the range of returns you're likely to experience, there would be a 70 percent chance that you would have enough money to live on for the rest of your life. In 30 percent of the scenarios, you ran out of money early.

For higher-net-worth investors, it doesn't make much sense to run Monte Carlo simulations based on having $1 remaining at the end of their life expectancy. Those scores would typically be approaching 100. High-net-worth investors normally want to accomplish more: leave a few million dollars for each child, fund their favorite charity, and so forth. Once those assumptions are built into the plan, the Monte Carlo score will provide the likelihood of success given their specific intentions.

THE "LIFE HAPPENS" PHILOSOPHY

Financial planning is all about living some version of your ideal, but all investors need a buffer between the ideal outcome and the real world. The reason is simple: Life happens. Taking the 70 percent rule of thumb too literally is a dangerous trap for investors. They might tweak their plans a dozen or so times in order to get them to the 70 percent level. Once they get there, they hand in their retirement papers and envision sailing off into the sunset. However, the year they retire, the market does poorly, and when the plan is rerun, they're actually at 62 percent. Then they realize they underestimated their living expenses in retirement, and suddenly they're at 55 percent. As you can imagine, those aren't fun conversations to have. These investors end up having to go back to work—and since not too many employers are chomping at the bit to pay a six- or seven-figure salary to someone in retirement, they could end up working at a wage that is significantly lower than they're accustomed to. Striving for a higher Monte Carlo score of 80 builds in a buffer that can help keep your plan on track.

For higher-net-worth individuals who may be invested in a wider array of asset classes, be more impacted by tax law changes, or have an expensive lifestyle with the intention of sustaining it throughout retirement, the objective is less about a particular score and more about minimizing risk in order to maximize the probability of success. Smoothing out volatility for investors with ambitious plans in retirement makes those plans more probable.

The Monte Carlo simulation makes it easy to quantify the benefit of "what if?" financial analysis. Consider it in baseball terms: an attempt to hit a consistent series of singles rather than swinging for the fences. Likewise, your advisory team will test numerous different strategies, trying to determine an approach that minimizes risk to the greatest degree. This might include tools ranging from tax planning to estate planning. If you plug different data into the software and your Monte Carlo score goes up, your plan is worth implementing. If you plug it in and the score goes down, it's not a valid option. This is an empirical, effective way to fine-tune a financial plan.

STRESS TESTING

One of the first things you learn in "financial advisor school" is that nothing ever goes according to plan. You can try to account for every variable and plan for every potential catastrophe, but stuff happens. So, in creating a long-term financial plan that might need to be viable for 25 years, you need to know how your plan will hold up when adverse events occur. That's why advisors do what's called *stress testing*.

You may be familiar with the term; it was in the news often during the financial crisis that began in 2008, when the federal government ran stress tests on the big banks to see whether they were healthy enough to survive. Financial advisors employ the same principle: Test your financial plan against a wide range of hypothetical adverse events to see how those events affect the results of your plan. What kind of adverse events? Try a litany of just about every financial nightmare that ever woke a stockbroker in a cold sweat:

» A bear market happens in your first year after retirement, in which the broad market drops by 20 percent.

» You suffer poor performance by a major component in your portfolio, such as your real estate holdings.

» Your spouse winds up in a long-term care facility. (Nationally, the average annual cost in 2016 of a private room in a nursing home was more than $92,000.[2])

» The business you own, which you believe to be worth $20 million, has several bad years and its worth drops to only $5 million.

» The top income tax rate rises from 39 percent to 49 percent.

» You find yourself subject to a large judgment in a lawsuit.

Once the stressors are applied to the Monte Carlo model, the simulations are run. If your score is too low after the stress test, it's time to begin strategizing ways to mitigate those risks. This could include any one of a number of strategies, from adjusting your future spending levels so you allow for slightly lower returns on your investments to tweaking your investment strategy so it delivers higher-quality income to utilizing tax shelters to increasing insurance coverage. A range of potential adjustments are applied to your financial plan, and the Monte Carlo simulations are rerun. The goal is to get you back to at least a 70 score—and preferably an 80.

What makes stress testing so valuable is that it allows your financial advisor to test your financial plan against the things that keep you up at night. The results let your professional team apply protective strategies before adverse events occur, so they can prevent big losses. After all, it's certainly easier to avoid losses than to try to recover from them.

The obvious benefit of stress testing is that it allows financial advisors to build more resilient financial plans that can better weather adverse events. But there are other, subtler benefits too. By running these scenarios by clients before they happen, advisors can desensitize them to potential losses. Behavioral finance research shows that people react with much greater emotional intensity to losses than they do to equivalent gains, and that can spell trouble for an investor. If an advisor's client is completely unprepared for risk and losses, when losses come (and they *will* come), the client is more likely to panic. Panicked investors are more likely to pull their money from markets, which only harms rates of return in the long term. For example, the annualized return on the S&P 500 from 1996 to 2015 was 8.2 percent. However, if you missed the 10 single best days of the market over that time period, your annualized return would drop to 4.5 percent. Six of the 10 best days occurred within two weeks of the 10 worst days. Staying invested is key!

Stress testing shows investors that losses and adverse events can and do occur, but that with planning and a cool head, they are survivable. This additional layer of sophistication helps keep investors from overreacting and makes it much easier for the advisor to steer a calm, predictable course through rough waters.

Stress testing can also reveal cracks in a financial strategy, something that is especially important when you're only a few years away from retirement. When you are in your post-work years and have shifted from the accumulation to the distribution phase, you're also more vulnerable to downturns and other adverse events. Even as a wealthy retiree who might have income streams from assets like rental properties, you have less time to recover from a big loss than someone who's 10 years from retirement. Stress tests can reveal those weaknesses so you can protect yourself before retirement rather than trying to do so after you've already retired.

FAMILY INDEX NUMBER

The final piece in this part of the financial planning puzzle is the Family Index Number, or FIN. Your FIN is the annual rate of return you would need to earn on all your investable assets—including cash—in order to achieve every financial goal you've set for your family. For example, let's say you have four major financial goals: to retire at 55 years old; to own vacation homes in Barcelona, Honolulu, and Melbourne; to send all three of your children to Ivy League schools and pay for their education all the way through graduate school; and to give a $1 million gift to the endowment of your alma mater. Of course, you want to do this while maintaining a comfortable lifestyle, minimizing your taxes, having insurance protection, and so on.

Your FIN reflects the annualized return you would need in order to achieve all those things within the chosen time frame. So if your FIN is 7 percent, then to reach all those goals, you need to realize an average annual return of 7 percent over the life of your financial plan. That's doable but not prudent, because if you look at historical data for the S&P 500 from 1950 to 2009, adjust for inflation, and account for dividends, the average annual return is 7 percent.[3] If you have a 20-year time horizon to work with and can tolerate some risk, a FIN of that level is manageable—although not preferred. How many people would sleep well at night knowing that 100 percent of their portfolio is invested in stocks?

Additionally, it's vital that your advisor consider the alignment of your FIN with your goals, your time frame, and your investing preferences. For example, if your FIN is 3 percent and you're a naturally aggressive investor who's comfortable with risk, you can afford to temper your aggressive nature. You only need to earn an average return of 3 percent, so you're better off going with a more conservative strategy that will preserve your capital. Your entire strategy should be to avoid strikeouts. You want to ride the baby roller coaster through the markets so when the inevitable bear market comes, you don't feel the effects to the same degree as a more aggressive investor does.

On the other hand, if your FIN is 9 percent and you're extremely conservative, you and your advisor will need to go back to the drawing board. A 9 percent annual return is an unrealistic expectation from a professionally managed investment strategy because getting that kind of return would require exposing you to an unwise level of risk. Possible solutions could be saving more, retiring later, or reducing retirement expenses.

Your life expectancy also plays an important role in determining your FIN. The higher the number you use for life expectancy, the more conservative the financial plan becomes, because the money has to last longer. It's typically prudent to go beyond the actuary tables when estimating mortality. Using an age of 95 when calculating the FIN accomplishes that. If there is longevity in your family, you might even consider using an age of 99! The point is, you'd rather err on the high side. If your plan is built based on you living to 97 years old and you check out at 94, your survivors will be a little richer.

Finally, not everyone has the same goals, and the FIN has to take your specific goals into account. Sure, many investors are determined to leave a substantial inheritance to their children. But some don't want to leave money to their kids, and others don't have children. Sometimes, these folks want their last dollar on their last day at age 99 to be a tip to the long-term care nurse who aided them during their final days. They want to spend it all, and their plan should reflect that. Other people might want to leave $10 million to their children after they pass away, and live off the appreciation and income that nest egg generates. For dedicated financial advisors, determining the Family Index Number means getting to know investors intimately, often tempering their expectations with reality, and in the end, helping them design a life. And that's a real pleasure.

IRREVERSIBLE MISTAKES

As mentioned earlier, comprehensive financial planning was designed to help you avoid irreversible mistakes. But just what are "irreversible mistakes" in the world of investing and wealth management?

Broadly, an irreversible mistake is any assumption or strategic decision that draws down your portfolio to the point where your plans are no longer an option. Since it's irreversible, it can't be undone. Barring a 50 percent jump in the market or some other one-in-a-million event, you cannot reach your goals. That's a hard situation for any investor to be in, and it's worse when you do it to yourself. No higher-net-worth investor, with all the tools and options at his or her disposal, should be in that position. So let's look at the mistakes a good advisor should help you avoid:

- » **Overspending.** If you're not budgeting and controlling your household spending, it can get out of hand quickly, especially if you live an expensive lifestyle. If you take years to get your daily spending under control, you could waste millions in potential gains that are gone forever.

- » **Missing out on opportunities.** Without a good advisor, you may not be positioned to take advantage of certain benefits of the tax code, such as removing future appreciation of your business from your estate. Here's an example: Maybe your business is worth $10 million today, but based on your growth rate, you project that in five years it will be worth $20 million. If you act now, you can move some of that increased value outside of your taxable estate, which will avoid estate and gift taxes. But if you wait three years to implement those estate planning strategies, the business might be worth $16 million and you might be able to move only $4 million of future appreciation into a strategy that avoids estate tax. So by procrastinating, you've increased your tax burden.

» **Failing to harvest tax losses.** You can take advantage of stocks that have underperformed by selling them and using the capital losses to adjust the taxes you owe. But if you wait too long, you might miss out during a tax year when you could really use the break, again increasing your tax owed. A good advisor will help make sure you time this money-saving method appropriately in line with wealth creation.

» **Improper asset allocation.** Without an advisor, you may find that you don't own the proper combination of assets necessary to maximize portfolio efficiency and achieve the goals of your financial plan. This creates unnecessary risk in your portfolio and costs you real money.

Those are just a few examples, but you can see the implication: Time really is money. The longer you wait to implement a truly dynamic financial plan that changes with the times, is tested against risk and adverse events, and reflects your family's goals, the more you risk not being able to achieve everything your wealth should be able to achieve. Even if retirement is a *fait accompli,* apply financial planning to the rest of your financial life.

Crossing the Wealth Line

» *Begin viewing planning as a process, not an event. Too many people focus on the deliverable of their financial plan, as if they're just waiting to get the green light to retire. Insist on better for yourself— greater wealth, not just hitting your retirement number. Seek continuous improvement in your affluence and financial security, year after year. Year-over-year progress is the metric that matters. Your advisory team should be tracking your overall progress, helping you spot potential issues before they can inhibit your success, and doing everything possible to counteract those issues.*

» *Make a habit of brainstorming with your professional team and implementing some of their recommendations year after year. This could range from seeking a higher-paying job to making changes in your small business that make it more saleable—moves that are likely to grow your wealth.*

A SMOOTH RIDE IS BETTER THAN A THRILL RIDE

People tend to like simple narratives, and no narrative is simpler than the scoreboard. We love sports movies because picking winners and losers is as easy as checking out who's ahead when the clock runs out. That's what makes films like *Hoosiers* so thrilling. The trouble with the scoreboard is that it's simplistic; it makes us think that the final number is the only reason to play the game. But if that were true, then we wouldn't cheer at *Rocky*, where the hero loses his big fight. We wouldn't cry at the end of *Field of Dreams*, where the game itself is secondary to lessons about time, magic, and family.

Sometimes, the scoreboard isn't the final arbiter of what's most important. If only more people remembered that when it came to their finances! As a society, we're obsessed with the "scoreboard" of the financial markets: the Dow Jones Industrial Average, the NASDAQ, the S&P 500, rates of return, and so forth. The Dow being way up or down in a single day has become front-page news; meanwhile, to the great majority of investors, pretax rate of return on an investment has become the only metric that means anything.

Here is a story that illustrates our obsession with rate of return: Joseph Kennedy, Sr., the father of John F. Kennedy, was a famously savvy investor who often talked about how he knew to get out of the stock market in the volatile 1920s before the crash that sparked the Great Depression. Kennedy said he knew the rampant stock speculation of the time would lead to disaster when he received stock tips from a shoeshine boy. When someone without financial expertise is giving you the latest "hot stock" tips, all anyone is focused on is rate of return, not the underlying quality of companies. That's your signal to head in the other direction.

This is not to say that rates of return are not important; of course they are. If you're in the Affluent or Middle-Class Millionaire group and still trying to put away enough money to have the retirement you want, you probably *should* be focusing on maximizing your rate of return. (But please refrain from taking tips solely from the average shoeshine boy, hairdresser, bartender, or taxi driver. Remember, if these people truly were financial prodigies, wouldn't they be likely to choose a more lucrative career?) No matter your wealth category, however, you should *not* focus on rates of return to the exclusion of everything else. Regardless of your income level or investable assets, you should also be paying attention to some other equally important financial questions:

» How can I reduce my income tax obligation as much as the laws allow?

» Do I have enough insurance to protect myself and my family?

» Am I planning sufficiently for my children's education?

However, if you are a higher-net-worth investor whose retirement is assured with the money you've already put away, your priorities are different. Once you've realized financial success, the fear of losing half of your money in the stock market should outweigh the potential benefit of doubling your money on this year's hot stock. In other words, once you've taken care of the future, your attention should shift from *managing returns* to *managing risk* and *minimizing losses*.

You're playing a different game now, one based on stability, minimized volatility, and after-tax, risk-adjusted returns. At this level, a smoother ride is more important than keeping up with the Joneses (or with the S&P 500).

SMOOTH RIDES, NOT HOME RUNS

Because your ultimate goal is managing risk and losses, over-exposure to one risky stock can do serious damage and turn a smooth ride into a gut-wrenching roller coaster ride. That's what happened with the Sequoia Fund. For years, this fund had been rock-solid, delivering a 5.7 percent annualized return from 2001 to 2010, while at the same time being 18 percent less volatile than the S&P 500 over the same span.[1] Over that same period, the S&P 500 delivered a negative annualized return of −0.4 percent.[2] That's pretty amazing.

However, Sequoia was heavily invested in Valeant Pharmaceuticals, a company whose growth strategy seemed to be not developing new drugs but borrowing money, acquiring other drug companies, and then raising the prices of their newly acquired products. For a while, it worked: Valeant's share price soared from $39.08 at the beginning of January 2001 to $257.53 on June 30, 2015, an annualized return of 13.8 percent. Over the same period, the S&P 500 delivered an annualized return of 2.43 percent.

Because of this, by mid-2015 Valeant had grown to represent about 30 percent of the Sequoia Fund's total assets. While that certainly would be considered an overconcentration to one position, critics were kept at bay as long as Valeant's stock was going up. But then, in March 2016, Congress criticized the company's pricing; lawsuits ensued, and the CEO resigned. When Valeant admitted that it might default on some of its debt, its stock fell by 90 percent. Through all this, not only did Sequoia not sell off its Valeant holdings—it bought *more* of the stock! As a result, over the period from Valeant's peak share price to its March 18, 2016, close at $26.98, Sequoia Fund was down 31 percent compared with a 1 percent decline in the S&P 500. So, with overexposure to a single stock, a mutual fund with an exceptional long-term track record of strong management essentially wiped away any outperformance investors had experienced over the previous several years.

Valeant had been Sequoia's home run. As most good managers know, when you're ahead in a game, your strategy changes. You go from hoping for home runs to striving for mistake-free ball. While home runs can be exciting, nothing is worse than striking out to end a game. Unfortunately, for Sequoia, they chose outsized returns over prudent risk management, and whiffed.

YOUR PLAN SHOULD MATCH YOUR GOALS

Annual return is a blunt instrument. Maybe you earned 8 percent on your investments last year, but what exactly does that mean? It depends. How much of that 8 percent return did you keep after taxes? How much sleep did you lose at night in the process? How much did you invest in areas that build your wealth or your beneficiaries' wealth? How much closer are you to your lifestyle goals? A raw return number can't answer those questions.

Your investment plan should align with your broader financial plan for the next 25 years . . . or more. It should be consistent both with your risk tolerance and your Family Index Number. It should free you from concerns about market highs and lows, and allow you to focus on the bigger picture of your life without letting a down market affect your mood. Simply put, your investment plan should make your life better.

Let's look at the chief areas your plan should address.

ASSET ALLOCATION

Asset allocation is the heart of any investment plan. It's a strategy that attempts to balance risk and reward by allocating an investor's assets among four primary asset classes: equities (stocks), fixed-income (bonds), alternative assets (real estate, commodities, private investments), and cash and cash equivalents. Each class has a different risk/return profile and responds differently to the respective stages of the economic cycle. By taking into account the investor's tolerance for risk, time horizon, and goals, the financial advisor can construct the optimal combination of assets to achieve the highest possible chance of achieving the investor's designated goals.

An asset allocation strategy makes how you divide your investments between asset classes more important than picking any one security. With asset allocation, integrating different asset classes into your portfolio is the most important element for reaching your objectives. This diversification will provide you greater benefits than focusing on a single security. Investors who are always looking for the latest hot stock are going to guess wrong a great deal of the time, no matter how good their information is, because markets are inherently unpredictable. Asset allocation is a proven way to even out the bumps in the market by diversifying across a wide range of investment classes.

Long-term data on market returns show that while asset allocation returns are never best in a given year, neither are they the worst. Most often they're somewhere in the middle. The idea is that asset allocation makes the roller-coaster ride of the markets more manageable. Anyone can play Monday morning quarter-back and say, "We should have been invested 100 percent in small cap stocks in 2013," but that approach is neither realistic nor prudent. As we look at the 15 years of annualized return data, it's clear that an asset allocation strategy provides the fifth-highest returns of the 10 asset classes examined, while having only the eighth-highest level of volatility. That's the beauty of asset allocation: *more return per unit of risk*.

YOUR IDEAL ASSET ALLOCATION

Your financial advisor will determine your ideal asset allocation based on a variety of factors that are unique to you. For example, let's assume you are a 60-year-old selling your business, and your primary emphasis is to generate an income stream to support your lifestyle rather than maximize assets for your children. Your financial advisor will probably invest most of your assets in a conservative mix of bonds and income-producing equities and alternatives. That way, a significant market downturn will have minimal impact on your income.

On the other hand, perhaps you are only 50 and trying to maximize risk-adjusted returns so you can leave a larger estate to your children or fund a private foundation. You have more risk tolerance and more time to recoup losses. In that case, your advisor might recommend a more aggressive asset allocation, with 60 to 70 percent of your assets in stocks and alternatives.

Asset allocation is the bedrock of financial planning, and

is grounded in modern portfolio theory (MPT), an approach developed by Nobel Prize–winning economist Harry Markowitz and introduced back in 1952. MPT is incredibly complex, and to explain it in detail would take the rest of this book and more. The basic idea Markowitz proposed is that the goal of any portfolio is to maximize the return given one's designated level of risk. In the context of portfolio management, *risk* is the volatility of a portfolio as measured by standard deviation.

Each asset class has its own specific expected return and volatility. Concentrated portfolios inherently create specific risks; the goal of asset diversification is to eliminate unnecessary volatility. Diversification achieves this goal because each asset responds differently to the respective stages of the economic cycle. Even assets that have a higher individual degree of risk can reduce a portfolio's overall risk because the high-risk assets move independently of the other assets in the portfolio.

Each potential combination of different asset classes has an expected return and standard deviation. The optimal combination of assets at each level of risk is called the "efficient frontier." Your advisor's goal is to create a portfolio of assets that lies on the efficient frontier but also is customized to your unique goals and risk tolerance.

MPT looks at your portfolio holistically and is dependent on historical risk/reward data. Because of this, not all advisors are fans of MPT. Investors sometimes feel apprehensive about adding assets that by themselves might have a high degree of risk, even when their presence reduces overall risk at the portfolio level. However, most managers rely on MPT because it has historically delivered consistent results while eliminating unnecessary volatility. It offers investors a quantifiable way to calculate risk and return, and it prevents the traditional dangers of "playing the market."

VOLATILITY MINIMIZATION

As discussed in the previous chapter, higher-net-worth investors should be worried more about hitting singles and doubles than about slamming a home run. Volatility is more than the variability of returns; it's the chance that you might not be able to achieve your personal objectives. For Affluent families, increased volatility might mean having to delay retirement. For High Net Worth and Ultra-High Net Worth families, increased volatility might prevent you from achieving your legacy.

The reason asset allocation is so important is that when executed properly, it eliminates unnecessary volatility. As a higher-net-worth investor, however, you should also focus specifically on your downside risk. Stress testing within a Monte Carlo simulation is one way to look at this, but from a quantifiable asset allocation perspective, investors should be focused on *maximum drawdown*. This metric looks at historical performance and measures the maximum percentage loss from peak to trough for a portfolio before it recovers.

Volatility is a necessary part of investing. Accepting that down markets will happen is part of having a disciplined plan.

However, proactively paying attention to certain metrics and creating steps to reduce the negative consequences of extremes is vital. The proper evaluation of maximum drawdown considers the huge downward market extremes that can prevent higher-net-worth investors from achieving their legacy. It's a useful tool when comparing multiple portfolio options that have a similar range of traditional risk/return metrics.

NON-CORRELATED ASSET CLASSES

When the value of different assets moves in the same direction at the same time (though not necessarily at the same magnitude), these assets are considered *correlated*. A correlation of 1.00 between two assets means they are moving in lockstep. Assets with a negative correlation means they move in opposite directions at the same time. This brings us to one of the key terms addressed in MPT: *non-correlated assets*. When two assets are said to be non-correlated, their performance is independent of each other.

In a good year, it's great to have your assets correlated because everything goes up and you make more money. However, the key component of prudent asset management and superior long-term wealth creation is to avoid unnecessary volatility and market extremes. During market stress, highly correlated assets will have exaggerated negative performance. Those extremes could have been canceled out by simply adding additional levels of diversification through the use of non-correlated assets.

Financial professionals determine correlation based on historical returns. After considering past performance, they assign two assets a correlation number ranging from −1.00 to +1.00. A correlation of 0.85 means that in the past, when one of the assets increased in value, the other asset did the same 85 percent of the time. A number of −0.50 means that approximately half the time, the two assets went in opposite directions.

Many non-correlated assets are what we call "alternative" assets such as real estate, commodities, and private investments. Some of these investments have high imbedded return and risk expectations; others have a volatility profile that's closer to fixed income. Whatever their individual risk/return profile, adding these assets in the proper mix can increase overall portfolio efficiency and reduce volatility.

For higher-net-worth investors, the addition of non-correlated assets is vital. Remember, long-term wealth sustainability is about more than trying to maximize return; it's about minimizing volatility and reducing the probability of having to change your lifestyle to achieve your goals.

Let's assume you are 65 years old and have $10 million in investable assets. Your goal is to maintain your annual lifestyle and gifting needs of $450,000 annually while leaving $5 million to your children or a charity. Consider these two portfolio options:

1. Portfolio 1, a traditional stock and bond allocation with an expected return of 6.50 percent and standard deviation of 14 percent

2. Portfolio 2, a portfolio with volatility-reducing alternative assets yielding a total expected return of 5.75 percent and standard deviation of 10 percent

Of course, you would expect the higher-returning portfolio to yield a higher future balance. But your goal is two-pronged: to maximize the probability of passing down $5 million and to minimize the worst-case scenario. The expected 30-year balance on Portfolio 1 is $17 million. The probability of having $5 million to pass down is 73 percent, and the worst-case scenario is that you run out of money in 26 years.

Alternatively, Portfolio 2 has a 30-year expected balance of $15 million. The probability of leaving $5 million increases to 80 percent, and the worst-case scenario is that you have a 30-year ending balance of $850,000 instead of running out of money. Higher-net-worth investors should be comfortable giving up a bit of upside potential in exchange for downside protection.

You're beyond trying to eke out every bit of return in a good year so that you can brag at your country club. Your concern is a smooth ride—and that's what the addition of non-correlated assets has the potential to provide.

ASSET LOCATION

This aspect of your financial plan addresses the taxable or non-taxable environments in which your investments are held. As you can imagine, tax minimization makes it critical that you hold the right investments in the right tax "wrappers" at the right times. MCMs and Affluents can focus on tax-advantaged accounts like IRAs and 401(k)s, but once your savings goals surpass the annual contribution limits, you need more hands-on management of your asset location.

You already know that some accounts, such as the Roth IRA, let you withdraw funds tax-free because your contributions came from after-tax dollars. Other accounts, like traditional IRAs, are tax-deferred; you use pretax dollars to fund your contributions, but pay ordinary income tax when you withdraw the assets. With non-tax-advantaged accounts, you're potentially taxed every year on your gains. It's essential to be aware of which accounts you're holding—and which you *should* be holding. Because, depending on your goals, not all accounts are created equal.

Let's say your advisor thinks that real estate investment trusts, or REITs, are the greatest thing since sliced bread and advises you to invest $50,000 in them. That could be a problem, because while REITs pay pretty good dividends, those dividends are taxed at the higher marginal income tax rate, not the more favorable capital gains rate that applies to stocks. It would be more advantageous for you to own that REIT in a tax-advantaged account than in a taxable environment. If your advisor hasn't recommended this, you're getting bad advice.

Let's assume you own a REIT in your nonqualified account. If you love the idea of the REIT as an investment, you can maintain the exposure in your portfolio while also increasing its tax efficiency. You can sell it in your nonqualified account, then repurchase it in your Roth or traditional IRA. You will still have exposure to taxes over the long term, but you're holding the asset in a more efficient place. Bottom line: Know where your assets are located, and make sure that your advisor understands the significance of asset location and that those tax wrappers make sense. Remember, Vanguard estimates that proper asset location can add 75 basis points of alpha annually.[3] That adds up.

LOSS TOLERANCE

As referenced earlier, research shows that losses hurt us emotionally more than gains satisfy us. That research, by psychologists Amos Tversky and Daniel Kahneman, found that this *loss aversion* explains the so-called endowment effect, in which we value something we own more highly than an identical thing we do not own.[4] Researchers Benedetto De Martino, Dharshan Kumaran, Ben Seymour, and Raymond J. Dolan demonstrated this in a practical way in a 2006 study. Participants each received $50 and were then given two choices: Keep $30 of the $50, or gamble the entire $50 with a 50/50 chance of either keeping it or losing it. Fifty-seven percent of the participants elected to lose $20 rather than risk losing $30 to keep the entire $50.[5]

When it comes to gain and loss, especially with money, people are not rational. Money and investing is emotional, which is why a large part of a good financial advisor's work is managing client behavior—particularly when markets are down. Before you sit down with your advisor to put together your financial plan, know your loss tolerance. How much are you willing to lose in the short term? How likely are you to panic if markets go down like they did in 2008? And if you do panic, how quickly are you going to call your advisor and order him or her to sell everything and put it in gold?

There's a saying in this business: *You make more bad decisions when selling at the bottom than when buying at the top.* Fear is a stronger emotion than joy or greed; when you're afraid, you make terrible decisions. Focus more on how much you're willing to lose than on how much you hope to gain, and build a financial plan designed to avoid going beyond that tolerable loss threshold. That way, you'll be more likely to stay the course until markets recover—and they always do.

RISK TOLERANCE

The performance of financial markets can vary widely over time. In my experience, most higher-net-worth investors are more interested in a smooth ride than in the thrills and chills of market fluctuations. Your financial plan shouldn't keep you awake at night, which is why your advisor should know your risk tolerance and plan with it in mind.

Risk tolerance is a function of both your willingness and

your ability to take risk. The beauty of a well-constructed wealth plan is that it determines your quantifiable ability to assume risk. Some investors have the ability to take the occasional swing for the fences while risking a strikeout; others need to choke up on the bat and take an easy swing in search of a single while avoiding strikeouts at all costs.

Your advisor will assess your willingness to assume risk through the use of a questionnaire and rate your personal comfort with risk as *aggressive* (knowledgeable about markets and willing to endure big drops in return for potential long-term gain), *moderate* (accepting some risk but balancing that risk with lower-risk assets), or *conservative* (more emotion-driven and willing to accept little or no risk of even short-term losses).

TAXATION

One of the most important ideas in financial planning is the saying *It's not what you earn—it's what you keep.* Taxes and inflation, while unavoidable, are also the biggest threats to your accumulation of long-term wealth for both you and your heirs. Markets will rise and fall. Litigation and other threats can be minimized with solid asset protection strategies. But as Benjamin Franklin famously said, "There are only two certainties in life—death and taxes." Both are unavoidable.

If you doubt the potential impact of taxation on long-term wealth for the wealthy, check out this example, originally posted on the incredibly detailed and insightful finance blog *Philosophical Economics*: An investor invests $100,000 in Altria Group on March 31, 1980, and reinvests the dividends. Had you done the same thing, on December 20, 2015 (the day this post went live), your investment would have been worth $93.6 million. That's a phenomenal annualized return of 21 percent. But, the writer supposes, let's say you live in wealthy Newport Beach, California, and you hold this investment outside of a tax-advantaged retirement account.[6]

At 2017 marginal rates, without considering deductions, your dividends would have been taxed at 37.1 percent: 20 percent for federal capital gains tax, 13.3 percent for California state income tax, and 3.8 percent for NIIT (the net investment income tax resulting from the passage of the Affordable Care Act). The impact of taxes means that instead of compounding at 21 percent, your Altria investment would have compounded at 19 percent. No big deal? Over 35 years, it's a big deal: The final value of your investment would drop to $50.6 million.

Yes, you read that correctly. Not holding your initial $100,000 investment in a tax-advantaged account would wind up costing you $43 million. That, as they say, is big money.

Now, you may never experience that kind of situation, but you will experience the effect of taxes on your wealth. Portfolio turnover—the sale of assets within your financial plan—creates taxable events. Holding assets like mutual funds in taxable accounts can eat away at your returns in ways you may never realize, especially thanks to high turnover rates. According to ratings agency

Morningstar, the 10 largest mutual funds, on average, sell nearly 75 percent of their shares in a typical year! With mutual funds, these taxable events are outside of your control. Other functions of certain assets, such as dividend payments and capital gains, may also create taxable events.

This is why asset location matters. Your portfolio should be designed to minimize taxable events—either by holding assets that create more taxable events in tax-advantaged wrappers or by holding tax-advantaged assets in taxable accounts. There are many ways to accomplish this, and that's where an experienced financial team, including tax attorneys and CPAs, makes a big difference.

ACTIVE VERSUS PASSIVE INVESTING

The matter of active versus passive investing garners as much attention as asset allocation when it comes to discussing portfolio performance. At a basic level, active fund managers will try to beat the benchmark that represents the asset class in which they're investing. For example, a large cap U.S. equity manager will attempt to beat the S&P 500. In some asset classes where information is readily available, it has proven to be very difficult to beat passive benchmarks. However, in asset classes where it is more difficult to research and access information (for example, emerging markets), active management can significantly improve risk/return metrics.

Active management is more than fund selection, however. It takes place at the portfolio level as well, and that's where the greatest benefit lies. Active management is used to determine how much should be invested in a specific asset class, which asset classes should be invested in, what types of vehicles are best used to access the asset class, and most important, what strategies can be employed to reduce the tax bill.

Higher-net-worth investors are more likely to be active investors—and that's as it should be. Most are more knowledgeable about the markets, but regardless, they still need active strategies. For example, the addition of non-correlated assets (especially private alternatives) improves portfolio efficiency. These strategies are inherently actively managed.

Higher-net-worth individuals also typically have the majority of their portfolios invested in nonqualified (taxable) portfolios. If that describes you, then your wealth manager should have a strategy for managing these assets in a tax-efficient manner and avoiding major taxable events (including mutual fund distributions). One such strategy that many investors use is owning a diversified group of individual stocks. These portfolios require active, additional oversight to monitor each position. Even more important, individual securities allow the use of active tax-loss harvesting strategies that can improve overall wealth creation.

A good active manager will know when to use active versus passive investment options and will judiciously utilize active strategies to minimize your tax bill while also remaining cognizant of the costs of trading.

RISK MANAGEMENT

Once your advisor understands your risk tolerance, his or her job is to effectively manage risk to give you the smoothest possible ride while preserving your capital. Remember, at the higher-net-worth levels, you're not chasing returns; you've already made your money, and you're trying to grow it prudently while avoiding the big bumps in the market.

Risk is a fundamental part of financial markets; you cannot have return unless you also have risk. There's no need to enter a long discussion of standard deviations and covariance, the likes of which probably would make your eyes glaze over. All you really need to know from a wealthy investor's perspective is that your financial advisor's job at this level is to balance risk with return and to reduce unnecessary risk. The goal is to preserve what you have, progress toward goals such as charitable giving and estate planning, and achieve consistent growth while keeping you on the kiddie roller coaster.

FOCUS ON AFTER-TAX
RISK-ADJUSTED RETURN

Finally, we come to the only metric that really matters: after-tax, risk-adjusted return, more commonly known as "real return." *Gross return*—your market returns before accounting for (1) the risk incurred in producing that return and (2) the tax you have to pay on your gains—is what everyone gets excited about, but it's not what matters for higher-net-worth investors. Why not? Because the majority of your investable assets are held not in IRAs but in non-tax-advantaged accounts. If you sell your business for $10 million but only clear $7 million because of taxes, that $10 million number is meaningless.

Asset location and tax planning can help reduce the taxes you pay on your investments, increasing your after-tax return. As for risk, every investor should aim to realize the highest rate of return given his or her designated level of risk. We call this "maximizing your risk-adjusted return."

Previously, we discussed one measure of risk-adjusted return—*alpha*—which quantifies the excess return a manager derives versus a designated benchmark. To recap, each individual security has unsystematic (company-specific) and systematic (general market) risk. Building a well-diversified portfolio can eliminate unsystematic risk. However, every portfolio has an aggregate level of systematic risk that cannot be eliminated through diversification. The *beta* of a portfolio, therefore, represents the magnitude of this systematic risk. A beta of 1 means the portfolio has a level of risk equal to the benchmark.

A portfolio with a beta of 1.2 has higher implied risk than the market and should have a higher expected return. For example, if the market were to return 10 percent with a 10-year Treasury bond yielding 4 percent, one would expect this portfolio to earn a return of 11.2 percent. However, if the actual return of the portfolio was 12 percent, then the manager had a positive alpha of 0.8 percent (actual return minus expected return). Most higher-net-worth investors are looking to reduce risk (in this case, beta) and would prefer to have a lower beta than the market. However, the amount of risk you are willing to take will depend on your goals.

Calculating alpha is a great way to determine manager effectiveness. However, it assumes that we have an easily quantifiable benchmark. As mentioned earlier, higher-net-worth investors often have a broader range of investment choices that may include assets such as private equity and venture capital. In such cases, their goals are not to beat designated benchmarks but to maximize after-tax wealth creation while minimizing risk.

THE SHARPE RATIO

Another way of calculating risk-adjusted return is the Sharpe ratio. It calculates the incremental return a portfolio has historically generated above the return of a risk-free asset, per unit of risk. In this case, we quantify risk by looking at the standard deviation—the variability of returns around an expected mean for the portfolio. We calculate the ratio by subtracting the risk-free return from the average return and dividing by the standard deviation. For example, if the risk-free rate of return is 3 percent, and the portfolio has generated a 10-year annualized return of 7 percent with a standard deviation of 12 percent, the Sharpe ratio would be $(7-3) \div 12$, or 0.33.

When evaluating 10 different asset allocation options, using the Sharpe ratio helps determine which portfolio option has historically generated superior returns per level of risk. The higher the Sharpe ratio, the better the risk-adjusted return. (For perspective, consider that the Sharpe ratio of the unmanaged S&P 500 over the past 15 years is 0.23.) Furthermore, anytime we add an additional asset, we can calculate the revised Sharpe ratio to confirm that the change improves risk-adjusted performance.

RISK ANALYSIS

Whew! That was a lot of information about what goes into developing an investment plan. It can be difficult to see things clearly when the concepts start to get esoteric. As you're probably aware, modern finance is incredibly complex, filled with baroque formulas and computer models that are tough to grasp for anyone without a PhD in economics. That's why you need a financial advisor in your corner. Work with one to determine your appropriate risk appetite and to design an investment strategy that helps you sleep at night.

Crossing the Wealth Line

» *Stop obsessing about gross returns. Reducing volatility should be your most important objective, even if you're not in the higher-networth groups yet. Chances are that your retirement strategy will call for you to draw income from your investments at somewhere between 3 percent and 5 percent per year. But withdrawing money in a down year can be devastating, so let's be honest: You'll give up a little upside in a good year to protect your downside in the bad years.*

» *The market has a positive year around 70 percent of the time. It's negative around 30 percent of the time. So with a conservative strategy that minimizes volatility, you'll underperform the market more often than you'll outperform it. That may not sound like a thrilling idea, but while your highs won't be as high as the others at the country club, your lows won't be as low either. This prudent investment strategy will help you sleep well at night, and your downside protection in the bad years will add a ton of value to your overall risk-adjusted return.*

» *Stop talking about the Dow and the S&P! You're not invested 100 percent in U.S. large cap stocks. Those are inappropriate benchmarks for you to try to keep up with. Ignore them.*

KEY #5:

YOU ARE YOUR OWN WORST ENEMY

A classic line from the movie *When Harry Met Sally* goes, "Everyone thinks they have good taste and a sense of humor." Likewise, everyone thinks they are a smart investor. But that's just not true. We're actually much more emotional and irrational about our money than most of us would like to believe. We're our own worst enemy.

During his time managing funds at Fidelity Magellan, Peter Lynch became a legend for his ability to not just beat the market but annihilate it, producing a 29 percent annualized return during his tenure. But that number was what the *fund* returned, not its investors. Lynch has said that during his time managing the fund, the average investor made only about 7 percent because when share prices dropped, investors quickly pulled their money out. When the ship righted, they would move their money back in, having already missed most of the gains.[1]

That's the impact of panic and irrationality. Time and time again, studies have shown that for most people, the best course of action is to build a solid investment strategy and then leave it alone. But we struggle with that, in part because we consume financial media. Richard Thaler, one of the fathers of behavioral economics, said in an interview that when someone asks him for investment advice, he tells them to buy a stock-heavy portfolio, limit their newspaper reading, and stop watching cable news altogether.[2] In the financial world, having too much information without context is worse than having no information at all.

Time and time again, statistics show that one of the areas where financial advisors provide the greatest tangible return for their clients is not in picking stocks or asset allocation but in behavior management—saving investors from themselves.[3]

YOU'RE NOT AS RATIONAL AS YOU BELIEVE

Money is an emotional subject for anyone, including you. You might believe that because you've accumulated a lot of assets and made your way into the higher-net-worth cohort you're more rational about your financial decision making than the guy socking away $18,000 a year into his company's 401(k). To put it simply, you're not.

That isn't criticism; it's fact. None of us are completely rational when it comes to our own money. Not even all financial advisors, who are compensated to be coldly rational about other people's money, are entirely logical when it comes to their own. The reason is simple: Money represents much more than purchasing power. In our society it means status, security, comfort, achievement. You need it not only to survive but to *live*. That's why, when faced with a stressful situation involving their money, many otherwise intelligent, reasonable people make decisions that defy even the most basic common sense.

Here's an example: Beginning in 2007, the global economy started showing serious weakness as the U.S. real estate bubble burst. Markets fell and consumers panicked. According to Thomson Reuters' Lipper service, people pulled $235 billion out of U.S. equity mutual funds starting in 2007, and many never got back in the market,[4] missing out on what became one of the most robust bull markets in history. In doing so, they defied the four most important words in investing:

Buy low. Sell high.

Why did so many investors defy this golden rule? Why did they buy high and sell low, and then fail to get back into the markets in time to catch the big gains? Because of fear and panic.

Keeping investors from making irrational decisions due to fear and panic is a big part of any financial advisor's job. Left to themselves, average investors make poor decisions that hurt them in the financial markets. They buy a hot stock when it's overpriced. They sell out of desperation when a stock is low. They engage in magical thinking that makes them believe they can time the market. The average investor is anything but rational. In fact, according to Morningstar, between 2004 and 2013, the average investor underperformed the average yield of the U.S. equity market, the international equity market, and the bond market by as much as 3 percent.[5] That's huge.

It gets worse. A study by Dalbar Inc., which tracks aggregate mutual fund flows, showed that the average retail investor from 1996 to 2015 had a 20-year annualized return of 2.1 percent[6]—well below long-term inflation and thoroughly underperforming asset classes like the S&P 500 and bonds. A 60/40 asset allocation strategy (60 percent stocks, 40 percent bonds) averaged 7.2 percent annually over the same time frame.[7]

What makes high-net-worth investors more successful is not that they are more rational than the average guy; it's that they *know* they're *not* more rational. They know that wealth is no guarantee against making panic decisions based on emotion. They know that if they leave their wealth management in their own hands, they'll harm themselves and their families. So they depend on dispassionate professionals who will make decisions for them based on data, not emotion.

That's the kind of investor you need to be. If you're already that kind of investor, this knowledge will help you become an even better one. So let's spend a little time breaking down some of the major ways that investors' behavior hurts them—and how your financial advisor can save you from yourself.

COGNITIVE BIASES

Paving the way for Richard Thaler, Amos Tversky, and Daniel Kahneman (mentioned in the previous chapter) were pioneers of the discipline known as *behavioral finance*. This field combines behavioral and cognitive psychological theory with conventional economics and finance, to provide rational explanations for why people make irrational financial decisions. Nicholas Barberis, Stephen and Camille Schramm Professor of Finance at the Yale School of Management, uses the tools of behavioral finance to understand the pricing of financial assets, and his findings shed some light on why investors act as they do.

Barberis has shown that by and large, investors make decisions for reasons that are not entirely rational. While many of us believe that we're good at making decisions and that those decisions are based largely on objective information and logic, that's actually a self-delusion. Most of the time, Barberis found, we make decisions based on intuition, a kind of cognitive autopilot. Then, after we make the decision, we rationalize it *after the fact* with data and facts that make us appear rational.

Researchers in behavioral finance have identified several important cognitive biases that compel us to make quick, often illogical choices while believing that we are being logical:

- » **Overconfidence.** We all think we're better looking and smarter than we really are.

- » **Loss aversion.** As the previous chapter pointed out, we give too much weight to potential losses.

- » **Short-term thinking.** We don't like thinking about the future, so we make decisions that are not in our long-term interest but instead satisfy short-term desires.

- » **Confirmation bias.** We look for data that agree with conclusions we've already drawn, and we ignore data that contradict those conclusions.

Each of these biases is a trap for the investor, and each is insidious because we're often not aware of it. Of course we think our approach is the best way! When you've had some financial success, that success can seem like a validation of your approach, when in fact a financial advisor might look at your results and see luck, or note that you might have accumulated 20 percent more wealth had you made better decisions based on data and not on your gut.

Bottom line: No high-net-worth investor should be a do-it-yourself investor. The stakes are simply too high when you have millions in investable assets, and the cost of mistakes is simply too great, both for your immediate returns and your family's long-term financial well-being.

BAILING OUT WHEN THINGS LOOK BAD

One of the most commonplace investing mistakes is taking money out of the market when it goes down. This is one of the most irrational actions an investor can take, and it's based on a misapprehension of the nature of the equity markets. It's based on four of the most dangerous words an investor can utter: "This time, it's different." Fear convinces some of us that somehow, this time the market is going to zero. We should buy gold, stick cash in a mattress, and stock up on ammunition.

But this time is *not* different. For all the fear about market downturns and fluctuations, the equity markets remain one of the best bets in the financial world—if you stick to a disciplined plan and don't engage in panic selling. For example, if you had $1 million invested in the S&P 500 on October 31, 2007, just before the Great Recession, and did not touch your money, on June 30, 2016, you would have had about $1.64 million—an annualized return of 5.9 percent—despite the fact that the S&P 500 lost over 50 percent of its value from peak to trough.[8]

Even with the collapse of the housing market and the failures of big banks like Bear Stearns and Lehman Brothers, the market eventually recovered. The people who stayed in the market recovered their losses and more, and that was especially true for those who had the wisdom to *buy* when the market was in a trough. (Remember—buy low, sell high.) Because they purchased shares at reduced prices, when the market came roaring back they made up all their lost ground and then some.

There wasn't anything special about the investors who stayed in . . . except that they didn't panic. However, the fact was that most of the people who pulled their money out of the markets between 2007 and 2009 were middle-class investors. According to the Investment Company Institute, while 53 percent of Americans owned equities through individual stocks, mutual funds, ETFs, and variable annuities in 2001, by 2008 that number had fallen to 48.2 percent, and by 2011 it was down to 46.4 percent.[9] Spooked by the recession, investors were reluctant to get back into the markets.

How do we know that it was mostly mom-and-pop investors who ran from the equity markets? We look at their wealth before and after. Federal Reserve data show that at the end of 2011, people with less than $100,000 in investable assets on average had $17,975 in their various accounts. That's down 9 percent from the end of 2007, when they had $19,732. Investors with between $500,000 and $2 million in investable assets gained 7 percent over the same period, going from average assets of $903,219 to $966,948.[10]

The wealthy did better during the downturn, and that's not because they're more rational. It's because they had financial professionals advising them and *preventing* them from making decisions out of panic.

Writing for Reuters, Jilian Mincer and Steven C. Johnson sum up the issue succinctly:

Investors who left the market at the end of 2008 or early 2009 paid a high price.[11]

Fidelity Investments found that individuals who had been investing for at least 12 consecutive years in their 401(k) plans but pulled out of equities in late 2008 or early 2009 had an average balance at the end of June 2012 of $167,000, compared with a $212,000 balance for those who didn't.

"The average investor tends to chase returns when things are going well and bolt when things are going poorly," says Drew Kanaly, CEO of Kanaly Trust Co. in Houston.

Preventing Damage

- Work with your advisor to develop a plan for down markets, and then stick to it.
- When markets drop, quit reading the mainstream financial press.
- Relax and remember that, historically, investors who have remained in the market have done much better than those who haven't.

MISSING THE BOUNCE

Volatility in the equity markets is like a tight curve in a mountain road: It's going to come, and when it does, the worst thing you can do is overcorrect. So-called corrections are normal events in markets, but when they occur, some investors pull their money out of the markets, intending to wait out the volatility.

This is how such moves usually play out:

1. A market index such as the Dow or S&P 500 declines steeply.

2. The investor panics and moves assets into "safe" instruments, like fixed income or cash, to wait until the equity markets recover.

3. The markets recover, but the spooked investor, now unsure of the market, waits to see if the "bounce" lasts.

4. Several weeks or months following the market's recovery, the investor moves his or her money back into equities.

Sounds prudent, but it's actually one of the worst decisions an inexperienced investor can make. By waiting until the markets are comfortable before getting back in, these people miss the "bounce"—the steep early returns that come when large investors, attracted by high-value stocks that are down from their peak prices, flood back into the markets. The fact is, missing just a few of a market's high-performing days can dramatically reduce your returns.

The impact of missing the bounce can be astounding. A study by JPMorgan Asset Management found that an investor who invested $10,000 in the S&P 500 and stayed fully invested from 1993 to 2013 would have realized an annualized return of 9.2 percent. However, if the same investor missed the market's 10 best-performing days in that 20-year span, the annualized return plummeted to 5.4 percent. That's the difference between having $58,332 after 20 years and having $29,111. Those 10 days literally *doubled* that investor's money![12]

Another reason to hold on to your "long position" is that

according to the S&P 500's historical data, some of the biggest one-day gains in that index have come the day after some of the largest single-day losses. Over the 20-year period ending in 2015, six of the 10 best days of the market occurred within two weeks of the worst day in the market. For instance, on November 20, 2008, the S&P 500 dropped 6.71 percent . . . and then on November 21, 2008, it climbed 6.32 percent.[13] Neither bear nor bull markets move in a straight line.

Preventing Damage

- Accept that volatility is a normal part of the markets, and be prepared for it.
- View lower indexes and stock prices as opportunities.
- Be aware of and understand the historical movement of the major indexes so you have some perspective.
- When the market drops, take it easy and ride it out.

EXCESSIVE TRADING

Another common mistake that investors of all kinds hang themselves with is trading too often. In general, when people trade stocks, they trade too many times. This is due to a wide range of causes: the desire for excitement, "grass is always greener" thinking (which suggests that the *next* stock will be the one that takes off), trying to "time the market," and so on. Frequent traders also incur additional transaction costs that cut into returns. And because they are trading hastily, often they select poor-quality securities without performing the necessary research.

In general, the more active you are in the market, the more money you lose. In a 2015 paper[14] for the *Journal of Economic Perspectives*, Kent Daniel and David Hirshleifer call excessive trading by individual investors the "active investor puzzle." They cite research by Barber and Odean[15] that clearly shows high-turnover investors—investors who trade with the greatest frequency each month—realize the lowest net annual return because of trading costs. In fact, their net return was about 30 percent lower than that of the investors with the lowest monthly trading volume. That's a substantial difference.

Research also shows that the stocks chosen by excessive traders tend to underperform. These high-turnover investors overrate the quality of their information, fall victim to the "winner's curse" (the phenomenon of paying a higher price for something out of a desire to win it or possess it), or simply become reckless because technology has made trading so easy and instantaneous.

But let's say you don't trade stocks personally at all. You leave all buying and selling to your financial advisor. Even so, you can still get burned if your advisor exclusively utilizes active, high-turnover money management tactics. According to a 2013 study by Vanguard, only 25 percent of actively managed mutual funds beat their respective benchmarks.[16] Why? The core of most investors' growth portfolios comprises major asset classes such as large cap U.S. stocks represented by the S&P 500. Information regarding the underlying companies in the index is readily available, making it difficult to find mispricings—under- and overvalued stocks. Without these mispricings, it is difficult to generate alpha. Without the ability to generate substantial alpha, the difference in fees between active and passive strategies becomes overly burdensome.

Furthermore, transaction costs include not just the actual cost of placing a trade, but also the tax consequence involved in selling an appreciated security. High-turnover strategies that generate increased capital gains, especially short-term capital gains taxed at ordinary income levels, detract from net-after-tax performance and wealth and are especially detrimental to higher-net-worth investors.

Active management is a crucial aspect of long-term wealth creation. In some asset classes where less information is available, there are persistent mispricings and active fund management can create net alpha. For higher-net-worth investors, owning individual securities can offer significant tax-alpha capabilities. Furthermore, active portfolio management involves not just picking securities, but adjusting the weight to certain asset classes based on market fundamentals, and determining when to use active versus passive strategies. However, there are no doubts that excessive trading is unnecessary and detracts from long-term returns.

Preventing Damage

- If you enjoy trading stocks, set up a small "play" account that you can use without impacting your larger pool of investable assets.
- Get your adrenaline rush elsewhere. Smart investing should be boring.
- If your advisor has you in actively managed accounts, know the expense ratios and how they are affecting your net returns.

OVERCONFIDENCE

Whether they believe they are highly intelligent, are extremely good-looking, have a wonderful sense of humor, are terrific drivers, or have inhuman acumen at picking stocks, people tend to have exceptionally rosy opinions of themselves. The trouble is, when it comes to stock picking, they're usually delusional. How delusional? Well, a company called Research Affiliates ran an interesting experiment. They selected 100 portfolios containing 30 stocks randomly selected from a group of 1,000 stocks, and repeated the random selection every year from 1964 to 2010. The idea was to simulate the actions of 100 monkeys throwing darts at newspaper stock pages (without the troublesome bananas and monkey poo). The results? The average "monkey" outperformed the S&P 500 by 1.7 percent per year.[17]

Still, millions of investors, mostly men, continue to insist that they can beat the benchmarks and outperform the broader market. Why men? Many would say that it's their competitive nature. Men evolved from hunters, and hunting the big stock payoff that no one else can find is an ego trip, so men trade more than women. This isn't conjecture: In 2001, Barber and Odean compared the trading behavior and performance of men and women and found that the average turnover for accounts opened by men was about 150 percent more than that of accounts opened by women.[18] Of course, men paid for this activity with annual transaction costs that were 0.94 percent higher—and realized lower net returns.

It's a chicken-and-egg question: Do naturally overconfident

people make worse investors, or do a few successes give investors a false sense of their own ability? Certainly, there's a case to be made for what's called "bias in self-attribution"—a concept researched by Kent Daniel, David Hirshleifer, and Avanidhar Subrahmanyam in 1998, and by Simon Gervais and Terrance Odean in 2001. Basically, investors who get big returns are certain that their performance is due to their general brilliance, making them overconfident and reckless. Meanwhile, investors who realize poor returns attribute them to bad luck, not to poor choices—and certainly not to overconfident behavior.

While we could debate the "nature versus nurture" question endlessly, one fact remains: Investors with an inflated sense of their own skill tend to trade more, and we've already established that people who trade more lose money. This was made clear by a 2009 study by Dorn, Dorn, and Sengmueller.[19] They surveyed 1,000 investors at a German discount broker and matched the responses to traders. Investors were asked whether they agree or disagree, on a scale of 1 to 5, with these four statements:

1. I enjoy investing.

2. I enjoy risky propositions.

3. Games are only fun when money is involved.

4. In gambling, the fascination increases with the size of the bet.

The researchers found that investors who agreed with these statements tended to trade twice as much as other investors. This backs up Finnish research that depicts frequent stock traders as "sensation seekers" like gamblers, seeking pleasure through risk and usually perceiving their skill level as being higher than what is shown by actual testing.

To summarize, overconfidence tends to make investors trade more often (leading to more fees and lower net returns), overrate their own skills and knowledge, and take credit only for their successes, ensuring that they don't learn from failed trades.

Preventing Damage

- Engage a financial advisor for regular "straight talk" sessions to remind you how difficult it is to beat the markets.
- Assign a friend or partner to be your conscience and remind you of past terrible financial decisions to keep you humble.

PAYING ATTENTION TO THE WRONG SOURCES

Remember earlier in this book those remarks that the sources of financial information who are most visible in the mainstream media—Suze Orman, Dave Ramsey, Jim Cramer, *Kiplinger's*—are not appropriate for the higher-net-worth investor? It bears repeating, because no matter what you do, you won't ever completely shut out lowest-common-denominator financial opinions. Even when you have a wealth management team handling your investable assets of $20 million, you will still see, hear, and read things that tempt you to make snap judgments.

Please resist that temptation. It's extremely important to follow a disciplined, predictable, systematic investment process, and that process doesn't include abrupt shifts in strategy based on something you read in *The Wall Street Journal* or on The Motley Fool.

In 2005, Barber and Odean confirmed the importance of not getting sucked in to buying or selling a stock based on media attention.[20] Their study found that individual investors tended to buy stocks that were talked about in the news, that were heavily traded, and that had yielded very high one-day returns. In other words, investors were susceptible to buzz and hype. Barber and Odean described this as "attention-based buying" and concluded that it came about because investors couldn't effectively research the thousands of possible stocks available. Overwhelmed by their choices, they used hype as a filter and bought what was being talked about.

The upshot, however, was that those attention-based stocks bought by individual investors tended to underperform stocks sold by those same investors. So the media attention convinced individuals to buy money-losing stocks that they might otherwise have never touched. The media gives much less attention to beaten down, undervalued stocks. They love focusing on the top-performing stocks, and by the time you hear about it, it's probably too late.

No matter how experienced an investor you are, you don't have access to the same information sources as a professional, nor do you have the years of experience to understand the implications of the flood of information on the market at a given time about a company and its stock. It's like a gifted biology student reading a medical journal: You might have the technical aptitude to understand the organic chemistry behind a drug trial, but you have no perspective on how the drug might affect clinical outcomes in real people. There is simply no substitute for experience and perspective. A good financial advisor knows not only what information sources to rely on for data and background on a specific company, stock, or fund—but what sources to ignore because they are either unreliable or irrelevant.

Preventing Damage

- Minimize your exposure to the mainstream financial media, especially the hyperventilating, "Buy this stock now!" kind.
- Rely on your financial advisor for accurate, up-to-date information from the real experts.
- If you want to read, listen, and educate yourself, that's great. Ask your advisor to recommend trade publications, websites, or podcasts that are frequented by financial professionals.
- If you really want to learn about investing, take some classes from a reputable financial expert.

THE DISPOSITION EFFECT

Ravi Dhar and Ning Zhu of the Yale School of Management have done the seminal research into the "disposition effect": the irrational tendency to sell winning stocks too quickly while keeping assets that have dropped in value. In their work, Dhar and Zhu found that most groups of investors exhibited this effect, which is basically the willingness to acknowledge a paper gain by selling a profitable stock while refusing to acknowledge a paper loss by holding on to a losing stock—essentially avoiding pain by not "locking in" the loss by selling.[21]

Interestingly, the research team also found that 20 percent of the investors they looked at had no disposition effect, and that the more sophisticated the investor, the lower the effect was. Low-income and nonprofessional investors were more likely to have a disposition effect, which supports the idea that greater education and the advice of financial professionals leads to more rational decision making, since higher-income investors are more likely to hire financial advisors.

The disposition effect hurts investors not only by convincing them to hold losing assets, but also by preventing them from enjoying the potential tax benefits of selling those assets and taking their losses. Remember, there is much more to buying or selling an asset than its direct impact on your gross return.

Preventing Damage

- Understand whether you have experienced the disposition effect.
- Work closely with your professional team to understand which assets you should hold, which you should sell, and why.

NO ONE IS RATIONAL

Doctors have their own doctors. Psychologists have their own therapists. And attorneys who represent themselves in court have, as the saying goes, a fool for a client. We are all too close to our own affairs to be entirely rational about our decision making, and here's the rub: No matter how much you think you're the exception, it's in your best interest to presume you're wrong. Because that's what will compel you to both engage a quality financial advisor and rely on him or her to steer your ship.

Remember, your financial advisor's main job is twofold: to prevent you from making irrational, emotional decisions and to be the steward of a disciplined, rational investment process. Choose the right person, and let that person do his or her job, and you will enjoy the smooth ride that you have been hoping for.

Crossing the Wealth Line

» *The best way to avoid misbehaving with your investments is to outsource your investment management. Hire a good financial advisor and/or money manager. Don't worry about underper-formance. Every manager will underperform from time to time. Different investment strategies will come in and out of favor based on the macroeconomic landscape.*

» *Look at your statements less often. Don't stress out over month-to-month fluctuations. Back off to annual assessments of your strategy—and remember that realistically, no strategy should be assessed over less than five years.*

» *Educate yourself. Read about behavioral finance and investor psychology. Learn about the realities of "the bounce" and why investors pull their money out of the market when they should leave it alone. Understanding your own decision-making process might help you make better decisions in the future.*

OWNING INDIVIDUAL STOCKS HAS ITS ADVANTAGES

Back in 2007, Warren Buffett set Wall Street on its ear when he bet that $1 million he invested in an unmanaged, low-fee index fund would earn higher returns than those earned by the heavily managed Protégé Partners, LLC, hedge fund. The bet doesn't end until December 31, 2017, but Buffett is already the clear winner. Through the end of 2015, the Protégé fund had earned a solid return of 21.9 percent—but Buffett's broad market index fund had returned *65.7 percent.*[1]

Buffett says he made the bet as a lesson, showing that the 2 percent to 3 percent fees often charged by hedge funds—fees that, as you've learned, can seriously impact net returns—are largely unjustified. That's an important lesson. The trouble is, the bet has also spread the myth that he who wants to earn a high return should just invest in index funds, mutual funds, and exchange-traded funds and call it a day. But as with most things involving finance, this one isn't quite that simple, especially where higher-net-worth investors are concerned.

Economics tells us that markets are rational, but real-world experience shows that they are anything but, at least in the short term. In the long term, markets do tend to value assets appropriately—in market-speak, a $100 bill dropped on the ground doesn't stay there for long before someone picks it up. But in the short term, investors can and do engage in deeply irrational behavior, leading to markets severely over- or under-valuing assets.

On December 5, 1996, then–Federal Reserve chairman Alan Greenspan addressed this reality in a famous speech before the American Enterprise Institute. In it, he warned that financial regulators should be watchful to see if "irrational exuberance" was artificially inflating the value of assets beyond what the rational market would dictate. In the context of the booming dotcom stocks of the time, his comments were prescient:

> How do we know when irrational exuberance has unduly escalated asset values, which then become subject to unexpected and prolonged contractions as they have in Japan over the past decade? And how do we factor that assessment into monetary policy? We as central bankers need

not be concerned if a collapsing financial asset bubble does not threaten to impair the real economy, its production, jobs, and price stability.... But we should not underestimate or become complacent about the complexity of the interactions of asset markets and the economy.[2]

Of course, Internet stocks were indeed grossly overvalued, and the correction that came in 2000 wrought some serious economic damage.

Alternatively, consider what happened with the smart thermostat company Nest, which Google bought for $3.2 billion in 2014. Or more to the point, consider what *didn't* happen with Nest. See, another company, Nestor, which sells automated traffic systems to the government and has been in receivership since 2009, saw its shares rise more than 1,900 percent after the deal because investors assumed its stock ticker symbol—NEST—belonged to Nest. Whoops.

So while markets tend to be efficient in the long term, bubbles and other short-term events can create opportunities—if you have the right guidance. In other words, the $100 bill doesn't stay on the ground for long. A good advisor can help you pick it up.

THE EFFICIENT MARKET HYPOTHESIS

Warren Buffett has never been a fan of what's known as the "efficient market hypothesis." The hypothesis says that the price of a stock always reflects all the available information that could impact that price, so that the price of a stock will always be its fair price. It also suggests that because stock prices rise and fall at random based on unpredictable market activity, it's nearly impossible to beat the market by picking stocks. But in a famous speech he delivered at Columbia Business School in 1984, the Oracle of Omaha eviscerated the efficient market hypothesis by pointing out that he and other highly skilled investors had significantly beaten index fund returns using an informed, value-investing strategy.[3]

In other words, there's inefficiency in the markets, and you can profit from it . . . if you know where to find it. In an inefficient market, according to the theory, some stocks are priced above or below their "true" value, which is based on factors such as their growth rate and future cash flow. Because of this, investors who can locate and select undervalued stocks can realize higher returns than people who buy into the broader market through index funds.

The efficient market hypothesis is still influential, but it's been heavily criticized because of the devastating effects of the financial crisis of the late 2000s. That crisis highlighted the main reason that markets are inefficient: They are a human enterprise, and humans are irrational. If people always made rational investing decisions based on data, then sure, markets would be efficient. But people panic. They play hunches. They commit fraud. They get blinded in hype or confirmation bias. They engage in behaviors that, on a large scale, can increase or decrease the value of a stock based on factors that have nothing to do with the health of the company. A market like that creates plenty of opportunities—even more so when your primary goal is after-tax risk-adjusted returns, not absolute returns.

This is not to say that you should altogether avoid investing in index funds, mutual funds, and ETFs. In reality, you want to cover all your bases and diversify throughout the market. However, the "index and walk away" approach represents exactly the kind of one-size-fits-all thinking that doesn't work for the wealthy investor. Instead, once you're in the MCM category or beyond, you should be more focused on holding individual stocks for the core of your portfolio and should complement these strategies with passive and active options where appropriate. Let's look at the reasons why.

VALUE OUTPERFORMS GROWTH

One of the most valid reasons for actively investing is that over the long term, value stocks are proven to outperform growth stocks. Okay, let's back up: What is a value stock, and what is a growth stock? Before we can move on, it's important that you're clear on the distinction.

A *value* stock is the stock of a company that is trading at a discount to its peers despite having similar fundamentals. In other words, it is undervalued and has the potential to gain in value—which, if you buy it when it's undervalued, increases your return. For example, back in the summer of 2012, venerable computer company Hewlett-Packard was considered a value pick because HP was trading at a 10-year low. However, smart investors who believed that the giant company had a valid turnaround plan were rewarded for their savvy: By the summer of 2013, Hewlett-Packard's stock had jumped in value by 72 percent—six times the increase in the Dow Jones Industrial Average.[4]

The key to identifying value stocks is finding companies that are undervalued while still being fundamentally sound, healthy businesses. Often, due to factors beyond things like cash flow, high-quality companies trade at a discount to their true worth. A company could have missed a recent analyst prediction for earnings per share. It could have launched a highly publicized new product that flopped. It could have recently lost a charismatic CEO and could be conducting a high-profile search. Any of those factors can temporarily exert downward pressure on a stock, making it a smart buy. It is important to note that just because a stock is cheap versus its peers on one metric, that doesn't make it a true value stock. True value takes into consideration quality.

A *growth* stock is a share in a company whose earnings are expected to grow at an above-average rate relative to the market or its industry. While such stocks are not undervalued, investors bet that returns will come from the company growing at a faster rate than the overall market.

Growth companies can be any size, ranging from small players entering new markets with disruptive technologies that can take market share, to well-run companies that dominate their market, such as Amazon and Starbucks. These companies simply outgun their competitors, own massive market share, and have plenty of opportunities for expansion.

So why are value stocks preferable to growth stocks, and why does that support the idea of buying individual stocks over index funds? First of all, historical performance data show that value stocks outperform growth stocks over a long time horizon, because value stocks are cheaper relative to basic measurements of value such as earnings. According to Brandes Investment Partners, a San Diego, California, money manager, the 10 percent of U.S. stocks with the lowest prices relative to their projected earnings outperformed the 10 percent with the highest price-earnings ratio by *9 percent* annually from 1968 to 2010.[5] That's value beating the pants off growth.

Value investors who do their homework tend to take their positions in these companies earlier, at lower prices, so their long-term gains are greater. Meanwhile, growth stocks are often high fliers where publicity and momentum have driven prices past the value of their future cash flow and earnings capabilities. Behavioral economics suggests that people will irrationally covet a stock when its price is going up, so a hot company will tend to attract more buyers even if its stock is overvalued, and investors will drive up its price because they demand continued growth. That's what causes bubbles.

High-flying growth companies also tend to be more volatile than value companies. True value stocks tend to be well-run businesses with sound fundamentals, while factors like greed and hype over IPOs can drive prices for growth stocks to unsustainable levels while creating unrealistic growth expectations. In other words, not every coffee company is Starbucks.

Passive benchmarks focusing on value stocks tend to base selection on certain *quantitative* criteria, such as price versus earnings, cash flow, or book value. While these metrics are critical for identifying true value stocks, they often ignore *qualitative* traits, such as the quality of the management team or industry trends, that define true value companies. In such cases, working with a financial advisor trained to identify value can significantly enhance long-term wealth creation. The best way to access this potential is by investing in individual stocks. This allows the advisor to identify such companies at the right time, and also provides the tax management flexibility necessary to maximize your realized returns.

TAX EFFICIENCY ADDS VALUE

Mutual funds are designed for retail investors with the goal of maximizing absolute returns in a diversified portfolio. Fund companies are trying to sell product, and in order to market any product effectively, they need to generate the highest returns. In order to accomplish this, many fund managers actively turn over their portfolios, generating short-term capital gains that are taxed as ordinary income. Most investors hold these positions in tax-advantaged IRA or 401(k) accounts, so there are no tax impacts.

However, higher-net-worth investors hold the majority of their assets in taxable accounts. These capital gains are paid out as distributions, and the amount the investor realizes is dependent on the size of his or her position—no matter when the investor bought the fund. You can see why this is problematic! The higher-net-worth investor, who owns a larger stake, will have a higher capital gain that is taxed at a higher rate.

Individual securities give a good financial advisor additional means to minimize a client's tax bill. Let's say you bought BuildCo Industries, a value stock, for $100 and it has appreciated to $200 in two years. It's a great company, but now the stock is trading at a premium to its peers despite the fundamentals. Your advisor wants to reduce your position in the stock, but doesn't want to generate a $100 long-term capital gain.

You also own WellCo Healthcare. You bought the stock for $300, but due to negative press coverage of its earnings report, it has fallen to $200. Your advisor believes that both WellCo and the industry are undervalued. So the advisor sells WellCo and realizes a loss of $100. With the proceeds of the sale, the advisor temporarily buys a healthcare ETF that WellCo is part of, maintaining your exposure to the industry. Then, in 31 days (because of the "wash rule," which will be explained later), you can repurchase WellCo stock while exiting the healthcare ETF position.

The WellCo transaction has given you a realized capital loss of $100 that can be used to offset your capital gain of $100 on the BuildCo stock. Your advisor can sell your overvalued BuildCo position and reinvest the proceeds into a different value stock.

The capital gain is $100, but because of the $100 loss in WellCo Healthcare, your net capital gain is $0.

This strategy has allowed your advisor to reduce your exposure to an overvalued stock, opportunistically invest in a new stock, and *pay no taxes*. Mutual funds do not give you the same flexibility to make these strategic decisions.

LOW-BETA STOCKS OUTPERFORM HIGH-BETA STOCKS

As explained in an earlier chapter, beta measures the degree of systematic risk (market risk) a stock has. The S&P 500 is considered to be the benchmark, and the beta of the market is 1. Stocks with beta under 1 have lower volatility than the market, and one would expect them to produce a smoother ride. For higher-net-worth investors who want that smooth ride, reducing overall volatility is a key goal.

Classic market theory states that greater risk equals greater return. But a 2013 study by Harvard University finance professor Malcolm Baker turned this fundamental financial theory on its head.[6] Based on a 40-year study of stock returns between 1968 and 2008, he found that low-beta portfolios delivered high average returns with small declines. This is a major anomaly in finance, turning conventional beliefs about risk-return upside down. Because it's so revolutionary, low-beta stocks are often undervalued—because, according to Baker, investors would rather pay more for riskier high-beta stocks for three irrational reasons:

1. **People prefer to gamble.** Psychologically, investors would rather take a steep risk for the chance of an enormous return than take a small risk for a small return.

2. **Overconfidence.** Investors believe they have the ability to reliably pick the next great growth stock.

3. **"Representativeness."** The comparatively small number of high-beta stocks that have paid off big, like Google and Facebook, cause investors to believe erroneously that the high-beta stocks they buy will do the same.

This pattern has been persistent. Some would argue that the outperformance of lower-beta stocks can be correlated to falling interest rates. Typically, lower-beta stocks are dividend payers, and the value of that dividend increases if interest rates fall. However, the fundamental goal for the higher-net-worth investor remains the same: to hit singles and doubles and not expose their portfolio to unnecessary volatility. High volatility, especially for higher-net-worth investors taking large normalized distributions, can be devastating. Lower-beta securities offer a way to reduce that volatility while still generating the long-term returns necessary to achieve their goals.

DIVIDEND-PAYING STOCKS DELIVER BETTER RETURNS

For the period from 1926 to 2015, the S&P 500 had a total annualized return of 9.8 percent.[7] Forty percent of that return was a product of dividends. However, dividends went out of favor in the 1990s during the tech boom. Investors turned to high-flying growth companies rather than more stable, dividend-paying companies. In more recent years, dividends have become fashionable, and they should be. The companies that pay dividends tend to be established and stable, with strong market share and good fundamentals. Consider some of the companies that have paid dividends to their shareholders for at least 100 years: ExxonMobil, Eli Lilly, Procter & Gamble, Colgate-Palmolive, and General Mills. These are businesses that are built to weather market shifts and changes in the economy and culture.

Dividend-paying stocks (specifically, dividend growth stocks) have historically delivered superior returns with less volatility. A study by Ned Davis Research compared companies in the Russell 3000 (a broad market index that includes large, middle-sized, and small companies) that have done the following:[8]

» Historically grown their dividend

» Maintained their dividend

» Paid no dividend

According to the study, over the period from February 2, 1987, to December 31, 2015, the following companies produced drastically different returns:

» Companies that *consistently raised their dividend* delivered 13.4 percent annualized returns, with a standard deviation of 14.5 percent.

» Companies that *maintained their dividend* delivered 9.4 percent annualized returns, with a standard deviation of 16.9 percent.

» Companies that *did not pay dividends* delivered 7.1 percent annualized returns, with a standard deviation of 24.4 percent.

In other words, companies that consistently increased dividends provided both superior returns and lower volatility. Dividend-paying stocks, in general, have historically offered superior annualized returns and lower volatility when compared with non–dividend payers. From 1927 to 2014, dividend-paying stocks outperformed non–dividend payers by 1.9 percent annually. Additionally, they did so with 39 percent less volatility.[9]

DIVIDENDS LIMIT MAXIMUM DRAWDOWN

Again and again, this book has reinforced the fact that higher-net-worth investors need to focus on maximizing after-tax risk-adjusted returns. However, proper risk management is about more than just maximizing the Sharpe ratio or reducing standard deviation. It's also about minimizing downside risk.

Huge losses can be difficult to recover from, especially if you're taking distributions. For example, Sarah has a $10 million portfolio of stocks and takes a $400,000 annual distribution—a perfectly reasonable 4 percent withdrawal rate. However, the S&P 500 fell over 50 percent from October 2007 to March 2009, and if Sarah was in the market during that period, her distribution would become $400,000 from a $5 million portfolio—an 8 percent withdrawal rate. That's not sustainable. By taking out such a large distribution, Sarah has less money exposed to the market recovery since she sold low to free up the cash for the distribution. One way to quantify this kind of downside risk is by looking at the *maximum drawdown* of a portfolio.

If you remember from an earlier chapter, maximum drawdown measures the maximum percentage loss over time, from peak to trough, before a portfolio recovers. Limiting maximum drawdown minimizes the negative consequences of a 2008 type of event. For the period ending June 30, 2016, the Morningstar Dividend Growth Index had a 10-year annualized return of 8.8 percent with a Sharpe ratio of 0.65. The S&P 500 had a return of 7.4 percent with a Sharpe ratio of 0.50. More important, the maximum one-year drawdown on the Morningstar Dividend Growth Index was 36.5 percent versus 43.3 percent for the S&P 500—meaning that the largest historic peak-to-trough decline in the Morningstar Dividend Growth Index was substantially lower than that of the S&P 500.[10] That's the benefit of dividend growth stocks. Historically, they have not only produced superior risk-adjusted returns, but also limited the downside damage.

There are three main reasons that dividend-paying stocks (specifically, dividend growth stocks) outperform their non–dividend paying counterparts:

1. **Higher-quality earnings.** These companies usually have been around for a long time and have produced consistent earnings growth.

2. **Financial discipline.** Companies that have a history of growing their dividends have better financial discipline. They are expected to pay a reasonable percentage of their earnings to shareholders while reinvesting the remainder into growth-oriented projects. This provides balance while preventing extremes. Companies that pay too large of a percentage of their earnings sacrifice long-term growth and fail to grow their dividend. Companies that pay no dividends often make poor acquisition decisions that are detrimental to earnings. The proper balance is key.

3. **Dividend yield.** In times of stress, dividends become particularly attractive to investors, and demand rises. In the low-interest-rate environments that typically follow a recession, some investors look at dividends as an alternative to fixed income.

MIXING INDIVIDUAL STOCKS WITH FUNDS AND ETFS

In giving you the reasons why individual stocks can deliver high returns, this book is not suggesting that you *limit* your portfolio to individual stocks. Quite the contrary, in fact. The more diversified you are, the better. In asset classes that are informationally efficient, adding low-cost, passive ETFs can add further levels of diversification and improve risk-adjusted returns. Furthermore, since most ETFs are passive, their tax impact is minimal.

However, in asset classes that are not informationally efficient, actively managed mutual funds can substantially add to risk-adjusted returns. For example, prior to the Great Recession, China was seeing double-digit growth rates while spending on infrastructure. In order to build infrastructure, Chinese businesses needed raw commodities such as oil and iron ore. Brazil was a major supplier of these commodities, which benefited the Brazilian economy and led to substantial profits for their commodity-producing companies. As a result, Brazilian leaders in oil and iron ore became a large part of the emerging market benchmark. A passive emerging market ETF, therefore, would have owned a large percentage of these companies.

The Chinese government is committed to building a more diverse economy that is more dependent on consumer spending rather than on infrastructure. An active manager might decide that the best way to play emerging markets is to invest in stocks that benefit from consumer spending in China and limit their

Brazilian commodity exposure. As we saw in 2008, demand for raw materials plummeted—and so did the passive emerging market benchmark. Skilled active emerging market managers limited their clients' downside exposure and drawdown.

This book has already discussed the benefits of adding non-correlated assets. Most non-correlated assets are what we call "alternatives," as described earlier, and while some can be accessed via ETFs, many that truly diversify are available only by investing with active managers. But when you're looking at U.S. large cap stock exposure, you will often achieve better long-term risk-adjusted returns by holding individual stocks. So it makes sense for most High Net Worth and Ultra-High Net Worth investors to add individual stocks to their mix of funds and ETFs.

To summarize, here are a few reasons for this that bear repeating:

» **You benefit from improved tax planning opportunities.** One of the issues with mutual funds is that if your fund is held in a taxable environment (not in a tax-advantaged wrapper like an IRA), even if you hold the fund all year and don't sell it, the buying and selling that goes on *inside* the fund by the fund manager can create a taxable event that you don't know anything about until you get a 1099 in the mail. Surprise! You may actually end up paying tax on stocks where you realized no gain whatsoever.

Here is an example: A fund contains IndustrialCo stock that the fund manager bought for $10 a share. You buy into the fund when the stock is at $30 a share. When the stock drops to $20 a share, the fund manager sells it. But while you realized a $10 loss on that position, you're allocated a gain of $10 per share, and you have to pay taxes on that! This sort of thing isn't a big deal for the Middle-Class Millionaire, who is normally not in a taxable environment. But it's a big deal for you.

Owning individual stocks also lets you more easily take advantage of "tax loss harvesting." When you sell a stock that has lost value before the end of the tax year, you can use that realized loss to offset gains and income, reducing your tax burden.

» **You have the opportunity to identify undervalued companies that you can buy "on sale."** If you have a savvy professional team, there are always opportunities to identify undervalued companies that are likely to experience less volatility in the future and that are trading at low price-to-earnings ratios. Those are the true value stocks that offer superior long-term returns.

» **You enjoy greater transparency in your portfolio.** This is largely a psychological benefit, but there's no denying the powerful impact that psychological factors can have on returns. Simply put, with an index fund, you don't know much about the performance of the individual stocks in it. Back in 2008, if you held the S&P when it was down 37 percent, you were more likely to be afraid of the market going to zero and thus to make an irrational, damaging decision.

With individual stocks, you know exactly what you hold and can review each company's fundamentals. Even if we faced a zombie apocalypse tomorrow, a high-quality company like Johnson & Johnson would likely continue to operate and make Band-Aids for the survivors! When you know what you hold, you are more likely to accept that while the market will overshoot and undershoot, over time it usually values companies appropriately.

» **You can implement options strategies on particular stocks that might be highly appreciated.** An option is a contract that gives the holder the right—but not the obligation—to buy or sell an asset at a specified price on or before a specified date. Sometimes people have concentrated positions in a stock or a highly appreciated position that they don't want to sell. In those situations, an options strategy might be appropriate to save them from a big tax hit while reducing concentration risk.

For example, a "collar" strategy could be implemented that would simultaneously purchase an out-of-the-money "put" option while selling an out-of-the-money "call" option. The strategy is complex, as it sacrifices major upside while limiting the downside risk of owning a concentrated asset. However, it can be a useful tool to prevent the realization of avoidable capital gains while still reducing risk.

» **You can select highly appreciated stocks to donate to charity.** Many people are most accustomed to writing checks to their favorite charities, but that's not always the best way to support charitable organizations or realize tax benefits. Sure, you could sell the stock, pay capital gains tax on the profits, and then donate cash to your favorite 501(c)(3). However, it is often more impactful to donate a highly appreciated stock and get a tax break, or to create a charitable remainder trust that benefits both you and the charity. That way, you get the capital gain off your balance sheet while still supporting a good cause.

The rules for doing this are pretty simple: If you own a security with unrealized gains that you have held for at least one year, you can donate it to a public charity and get a tax deduction for the full fair market value of the security, up to 30 percent of your adjusted gross income. If the stock has seen strong appreciation, the savings could be substantial.

» **Your estate planning strategies become more effective.** It can be easier to create an estate plan around individual stocks than it is using the assets in a fund.

The upshot of all this is that the efficient market isn't so efficient after all. Work with your advisory team to develop a strategy to take advantage of the market's inefficiency and you're more likely to see real benefits.

Crossing the Wealth Line

» *Consider building a portfolio of dividend-paying stocks as a component of any prudent investment strategy. These stocks offer better risk-adjusted returns and better performance with less volatility. Consider dividend aristocrat ETFs and mutual funds as additional options.*

» *The dividend yield will help generate the cash flow that you'll need in retirement. This will help you in a down year. You won't be forced to sell your stocks while they're low to generate cash. You can simply withdraw the dividends.*

THE 60/40 PORTFOLIO SPLIT IS DEAD

Bonds are the most common fixed income investments and a core component of any well-diversified portfolio. They are synonymous with safe, conservative investing. Typically, the goal of fixed income investing is to provide predictable income and principal protection. According to conventional wisdom, bonds are safe investments that will always go up and that never, ever lose value. But as we're going to see, that conventional wisdom is false.

Since 1982, bonds have filled their role as the foundation of portfolio safety with admirable predictability, due in part to a decreasing interest-rate environment. We have been in a bond bull market for multiple economic cycles as U.S. growth and productivity have slowed and interest rates have fallen. For example, in 1982, the Federal Reserve lowered the federal funds rate from

15 percent (it's difficult to grasp that rates were once that high!) to 8.5 percent. In September 1992, the Fed lowered the rate to 3 percent. Since then, it has not risen above 6.5 percent, and since April 2008, the rate has been below 2 percent—and has dipped as low as zero.[1]

During this time, bonds have appreciated considerably. Why? Because as interest rates go down, bond prices go up. Thus, millions of investor portfolios have been structured around a 60/40 split in which the portfolio consists of 60 percent stocks and 40 percent bonds. For most of that time, that allocation has served investors well. In 1980, the 10-year Treasury yield was at 11.1 percent.[2] The P/E ratio of the S&P 500 was 7.4.[3] At those levels, both stocks and bonds were priced to deliver excellent returns, and they did.

In 2017, however, conditions have changed. Interest rates are increasing, albeit slowly. The Treasury yield is under 3 percent,[4] and the P/E ratio of the S&P 500 is above 20.[5] These indicators suggest that both stocks and bonds have become more expensive and will likely deliver lower returns in the future. During years of negative stock market performance, bonds have typically buoyed investors' portfolios. But unfortunately, when interest rates begin to go back up, bond prices typically come down. This means that a traditional 60/40 portfolio management and asset allocation strategy is no longer as effective as it has been in the past. Investors and financial advisors alike need to bring our thinking into greater alignment with the current market conditions.

BONDS DO SHOW NEGATIVE RETURNS

As prudent investors know, looking forward, not backward, is what matters when it comes to performance and portfolio optimization. The trouble is that many investors' longstanding view of bonds—that they always go up—does not correlate with the current state of the bond market. In fact, investors can and do lose money in bonds. The general bond index (Barclays Aggregate) has had years of negative performance, such as 2013 when it was down 2 percent.[6] Furthermore, if you were to look at five-year rolling annualized returns of the general bond index for the period 1950–2015, you would see that the worst five-year annualized return on bonds was negative 3 percent.[7] While those examples may not be significantly negative, they do prove that bonds don't always go up.

Complacency is one of the reasons to be wary of bonds as automatic safe havens. Low interest rates and cheap debt have powered high bond values in the past, but they also encourage bond issuers—especially businesses—to take on historically high amounts of debt. This fact is evident in the minutes from the Federal Reserve's September 2016 meeting:

> A few participants expressed concern that the protracted period of very low interest rates might be encouraging excessive borrowing and increased leverage in the non-financial corporate sector.[8]

In the carefully calibrated language of the financial world, that is an expression of alarm. Later, the U.S. Office of Financial Research issued its own statement on the debt market:

> Credit risks remain elevated in U.S. non-financial businesses. The ratio of debt to earnings among firms has also approached or exceeded peak levels from past credit cycles, even for borrowers with investment-grade ratings.[9]

With financial regulators increasingly concerned about huge debt loads and their potential to trigger chaotic financial events, it becomes increasingly likely that the Federal Reserve will further increase interest rates, which most often drives down bond prices. So now, perhaps more than at any time in the past three decades, higher-net-worth investors should beware of complacency about bonds, and instead actively work with their advisory teams to develop new strategies to smooth their ride.

WHAT IS A BOND?

Before we look at how to do this, a quick refresher course on bonds will be helpful.

Unlike stocks, which represent a form of ownership in a corporation, bonds are debt. You are lending money to an entity such as the U.S. government, a municipality, or a private corporation. For a typical bond, you lend money (the principal or face value) for a designated time (maturity) and earn periodic interest (coupon). Once the bond has matured, you are paid back the initial principal. If you buy a bond on the secondary market, the amount you pay may be more or less than the face value.

As a vehicle that a wide range of entities can use to raise capital, bonds are highly democratic. That means that while Ryan Gosling's character in *The Big Short* may have derided bonds in the 1970s as boring, they're really not. Startup businesses, celebrities, and even homeless shelters have tapped in to the bond markets to get money to take on desired projects. Here are some examples of less-than-dull bonds:[10]

» The London-based Mexican fast-food chain Chilango sold one million British pounds' worth of bonds through crowdfunding website Crowdcube. The so-called burrito bond (which featured a substantial coupon of 8 percent) included two vouchers for free burritos for investors who bought 500 pounds in bonds. Investors who purchase 10,000 pounds, however, might end up weighing 10,000 pounds: They're entitled to eat free at the chain once a week throughout the four-year maturity of the bonds.

» In 1997, music superstar David Bowie issued bonds whose debt was backed by future royalties earned by the 25 albums he had recorded before 1990. The 10-year bond also had pretty generous terms, with a 7.9 percent coupon over 10 years. The bond issue paid off, too: Bowie gained $55 million and used the capital to buy back the rights to songs from his catalog owned by third parties.

» You can also buy "catastrophe bonds" from insurance companies. These bonds give you regular payments—unless a natural disaster hits, in which case they lose value. They are normally issued as bets against conventional disasters like hurricanes, wildfires, and earthquakes, but in 2013 the United Services Automobile Association sold *meteor bonds*. These bonds will lose value only if large extraterrestrial bodies such as meteors or comets actually threaten to strike the earth and inflict the kind of serious damage generally seen in movies like Michael Bay's *Armageddon*.

Bonds have been sold to raise funds to cover a huge range of proposed expenditures, from building golf courses to raising $40 million to build an artificial sweetener manufacturing plant in a small Missouri town. The point is that while bonds may seem predictable, boring, and therefore utterly safe, they are like every other class of investment: subject to different and changing levels of risk depending on underlying conditions.

Most investors access bonds via mutual funds or ETFs (though, as you will soon learn, higher-net-worth investors should use individual bonds if possible). These are the major classes of bonds:

» Government bonds (such as U.S. Treasuries)

» Mortgage- or asset-backed securities

» Municipal bonds

» Corporate bonds

» International bonds (government or corporate)

» High-yield bonds (non-investment-grade municipal or corporates)

The income payments for each of these different bond classes varies. Each class of bond is unique, with its own specific characteristics and risks, and fixed income returns depend on the structure of the bond and prevailing market conditions. Also, most bonds are taxed at the ordinary marginal income tax rate. However, U.S. Treasury bonds are state tax exempt whereas municipal bonds are typically exempt from both state and federal taxes. As you can imagine, the location of these assets—in qualified or non-tax-advantaged accounts—can be of vital importance for higher-net-worth investors.

WHAT AFFECTS BOND VALUE?

It's already clear that bonds are not quite as simple as many investors believe, and the same is true of increases and decreases in their value. Despite the adage that claims when interest rates go up, bond prices go down (and vice versa), unfortunately it is much more complicated than that. Bonds are subject to several types of risk:

» Interest rate

» Inflation

» Reinvestment

» Credit or default

» Liquidity

» Spread

» Optionality

Interest rate risk is fairly easy to understand. When interest rates change, the value of interest rate payments becomes more or less valuable. Let's say you buy, for $1,000, a 10-year Treasury bond yielding 3 percent. But later in the year the Federal Reserve increases the Federal Funds Rate, and now investors can buy a 10-year Treasury bond yielding 4 percent. Your bond has become less valuable; if you tried to sell it, you would no longer receive $1,000. You might be able to get only $920. That bond is now trading at a *discount*. The interest rate environment is probably the single biggest risk involved with prudent fixed income investing.

Writing in *Forbes*, Sean Hanlon—chairman, CEO, and chief investment officer of Hanlon Investment Management—describes the reality of rate changes in no uncertain terms:

> It is amazing how much of an impact a small increase in interest rates can have on your hard-earned principal. . . . In [one] example, the interest rate on the 10-year U.S. Treasury note fell and then moved up 0.35 percent in just one morning. While this was an outlier event, it

does show that rates can move rapidly if market views on interest rates change suddenly.[11]

Interest rate risk is also affected by *duration*, a measurement of the amount of years it takes for the price of a bond to be repaid by its cash flows. The duration is also the approximate percentage change in a bond's price given a 100-basis point (1 percent) change in market interest rates. Let's say that instead of a 10-year bond, you bought a five-year bond yielding 2 percent. Now that same bond can be bought on the open market for 3 percent. Your bond will still trade at a discount, but instead of $920, it is trading for $960. Why the difference, when interest rates changed 1 percent in both scenarios? Because the price of the bond is affected by the duration. If you're locked in to a bond for a longer period, receiving smaller payments than you could get on the open market, the price of your bond will be more adversely affected. On the other hand, if the prevailing market rates were to fall, having a longer duration would be good.

Inflation is related to interest rate risk. The Federal Reserve's primary mission is to control the rate of inflation by tightening or loosening the money supply. Its main tool for doing this is the federal funds rate—the interest rate financial institutions use to lend money to each other. When inflation is a concern, often the Fed will raise the federal funds rate, which in turn will reduce bond yields. Additionally, the real risk here is that your earnings won't keep up with inflation. If inflation is running at 4 percent and your bonds are earning 3 percent annually, you're losing purchasing power.

Credit risk is the potential that an issuer will default. U.S. government bonds are considered to be 100 percent risk-free. However, as you go from U.S. Treasuries to other government entities to corporations, the ability to repay debt decreases—and so does the subsequent credit quality. In order for you to invest in lower-quality entities with a higher default risk, you need to be compensated at a higher rate.

The bottom line: Bonds are not necessarily the risk-free havens that many investors believe them to be. But even in an environment where interest rates are rising and bond yields are more volatile, bonds can still be an important component of a well-designed portfolio.

INVESTING IN BONDS WISELY

As discussed, investors need to be aware of the specific risks that are involved in investing bonds. These risks revolve around not just the specific characteristics of bonds, but how one accesses them; how an investor gains exposure to bonds is important. Most investors access bonds via mutual funds or ETFs, and while this is a great tool for diversification, it can potentially increase risk.

Here's why: The *yield to maturity* of a bond is the annualized total return of the bond when you hold it to maturity. Even if you pay more than the face value, the combination of income and principal repayment would generate a positive return as measured by that yield to maturity. However, if you sold that bond before maturity, you could gain or lose money on your investment, depending on prevailing market conditions.

Your intention in buying a bond should be to hold it to maturity, and when you own individual bonds, their maturity date is fixed. But with a mutual fund or an indexed ETF, there is no set maturity. The fund is meant to be run in perpetuity. For example, let's say you need to withdraw $100,000 from your fixed income portfolio in five years. You buy a five-year bond with a yield to maturity of 2 percent and get your principal back in five years. No matter what happens to the interest rate environment, you will get your 2 percent return and principal back at maturity (unless you bought a low-quality bond that defaults).

But what if your fixed income assets are in a bond fund, and you need to liquidate $100,000 of that bond fund at a time when the interest rate environment has increased by 200 basis points, risk assets have sold off, and spreads have increased? You'll be selling at a distressed price, and you can lose principal. Managing the duration of the portfolio of funds is one tool that can help mitigate this risk, but it is still less effective than owning a bond directly.

The other issues that make bond funds less ideal for higher-net-worth individuals are transparency and credit risk. In our previous example, what if the bond fund you owned was an actively managed tactical income fund? That fund has the right to own 40 percent of its assets in non-investment-grade credit—higher-risk, more volatile bonds with a higher yield but a higher chance of default. Wait a second! In buying this fund, you thought you were investing into a low-volatility, core fixed-income fund. Now your entire portfolio risk exposure has changed.

50/30/20 IS THE NEW 60/40

Regardless of how you choose between individual bonds and bond funds, the fact remains that rising interest rates have made the conventional 60/40 portfolio composition obsolete for many higher-net-worth investors. It's time to rethink that traditional strategy by adding alternatives and other non-correlated asset classes such as hedge funds, private equity, and real estate.

Because of the changing circumstances in the market, many higher-net-worth investors are now considering a new alternative to the 60/40 split: 50/30/20. This represents a portfolio that consists of 50 percent equities, 30 percent fixed income (bonds), and 20 percent alternatives such as managed futures, derivatives, and commodities. This provides added diversification, minimizes drawdown, and increases risk-adjusted return. Managed prudently, this new portfolio mix can reduce overall volatility and offer the smooth ride you're looking for.

Here are two more sound pieces of bond-related advice:

» **Understand what you own.** If you aren't sure what blend of individual bonds, bond funds, and ETFs you own, find out. The kind of fixed-income assets held in your portfolio can have a profound impact on your ability to extract the value you need when it comes time to sell.

» **Pay attention to the tax status of any bond income payments.** Different kinds of bonds are subject to different levels of taxation. The interest paid on U.S. government bonds is tax-free at the federal level, but taxable at the federal level. The interest from municipal bonds is federally tax-free and potentially state and local tax-free, as well. Meanwhile, interest on corporate bonds is taxable at all levels. For example, an investor who owns 50 corporate bonds with a par value of $1,000, each paying 5 percent annually, would expect to receive $2,500 of taxable interest each year and is required to declare that income on his or her personal income tax return. Remember, you are focused on after-tax wealth creation, not absolute yield. It's important to pay attention to the tax implications of your bond holdings.

So often in financial markets, investor problems can be traced back to the *presumption of absolutes*: believing that investments or market conditions are always stable and can be understood in black and white terms. But as reality shows, they are neither. Market conditions that affect investment performance are dynamic and fluid, changing not just from day to day but from moment to moment. Everything is relative, including the safety and predictability of bonds. They remain important parts of a diversified portfolio, but as the environment changes, your strategy must change with it.

Crossing the Wealth Line

» *If you're in the Affluent or MCM group, your portfolio is probably not large enough to build a diversified portfolio of individual bonds. Therefore, stick with low-cost ETFs and indexed funds that mimic the Barclays Aggregate Bond Index. Consider adding international and emerging market bond exposure through active fund managers with a good track record.*

» *Consider being conservative about adding alternatives to your portfolio; start with 10 percent in alternatives rather than 20 percent, for a 55/35/10 mix of assets. Bonds could be a headwind to performance over the next several years, so finding other non-correlated investments will become more and more important.*

KEY #8:

DON'T FEAR THE HEDGE FUND (OR OTHER ALTERNATIVE ASSET CLASSES)

The previous chapter discussed the benefits of adding non-correlated assets. For one thing, their performance is independent and doesn't move in tandem with the broader markets. Plus, when combined with traditional stocks and bonds, they reduce overall portfolio volatility and maximize risk-adjusted returns. But what exactly is a non-correlated asset? Let's look at some answers.

MYTH-BUSTING ALTERNATIVE ASSET CLASSES

Take hedge funds, one of the best-known non-correlated asset classes. Most investors think of hedge funds, which have become infamous over recent years due to the Bernie Madoff scandal and the failure of Long-Term Capital Management, as extremely risky investments. They charge unusually high fees (though the average fee has dropped from 1.68 percent to 1.39 percent over the past decade)—often a percentage of assets under management as well as a percentage of the upside profit—and have specific risks, including the use of leverage, limited transparency, concentrations, and low liquidity. Furthermore, most have underperformed general market indices during the recovery from the Great Recession.

That certainly doesn't sound appealing, but there are a lot of myths to bust. First of all, not all private investments, hedge funds, and alternatives are the same. Each alternative asset class and strategy has its role in a diversified portfolio and can be accessed via multiple structures. Let's review a few of these asset classes and specific strategies to gain some context:

1. **Real estate.** Primarily involves funds or companies that specialize in owning and operating income producing real estate. Investment can be made via publicly traded vehicles such as real estate investment trusts (REITs) or private funds.

2. **Commodities.** Funds that invest in commodities such as precious metals, energy, and agriculture. Exposure is typically gained via public funds that invest in futures contracts.

3. **Long/short.** A strategy historically utilized by hedge funds (although there are now publicly traded options). The manager shorts (sells) a security it perceives to be overvalued without actually owning it, then goes long (buys) an undervalued security. The goal is for the longs to outperform the shorts. At a future period, the manager must purchase and deliver the security it has shorted. A long/short can have a net long, short, or market-neutral bias.

4. **Multi-strategy or absolute return.** Often utilized by hedge funds. The manager has the flexibility to utilize multiple alternative strategies such as global macro, long/short, arbitrage, distressed credit, and so forth, with the goal of delivering absolute positive return in both up and down markets. Each of the underlying strategies utilized by an absolute return manager also represents a separate class of hedge fund strategies.

5. **Managed futures.** A fund (either publicly traded or private) that primarily uses trend-following signals to long/short futures contracts. These contracts can include multiple asset classes such as currencies, commodities, and equities.

6. **Private equity.** Accessed via private funds. The goal is to directly invest in companies that are not public. The purpose of investment is to maximize the value of the company,

whether that means injecting capital to promote expansion, replacing management to improve operations, or utilizing cheaper debt to sell pieces of the company for a higher aggregate price.

Hedge funds and alternative investments can be great complementary pieces of a higher-net-worth investor's portfolio strategy. However, since the media tends to focus on the strikeouts and home runs, there's a misperception that all hedge funds are risky. For example, Long-Term Capital Management (LTCM) was a headline grabber that still leaves a bad taste in the public's mouth. LTCM was a hedge fund that at its peak in 1998 had about $4.7 billion in assets, controlled more than $100 billion, and had investments worth more than $1 trillion.[1] The fund had produced annualized returns of 21 percent, 43 percent, and 41 percent in its first three years. However, LTCM was highly leveraged, and when global financial problems led to huge losses, the fund was near default on its debts. In 1998, LTCM lost $4.4 billion of its $4.7 billion in capital. The situation was so dire that if LTCM, whose holdings represented about 5 percent of the global bond market, had defaulted, it could have triggered a worldwide financial collapse.

On the home run side, we go back to *The Big Short*, whether you prefer Michael Lewis's nonfiction book or the movie version. Michael Burry, a physician who quit medicine to start his Scion Capital hedge fund, became famous for identifying the default risk of mortgage-backed securities and shorting them, eventually earning a 489.34 percent return for his investors.[2] But those are *outliers*. Most hedge funds are neither historic failures nor epic winners. For a higher-net-worth investor's portfolio, the best fits tend to be those that fly under the radar—the ones that aren't swinging for the fences but rather are designed to provide smooth, non-correlated returns, with a strong emphasis on risk management.

BENEFITS OF INCORPORATING ALTERNATIVE ASSET CLASSES

Let's take a look at how a portfolio incorporating some of these asset classes performs versus a more traditional portfolio. First, the traditional stock/bond portfolio: According to Morningstar, for the 10-year period ending August 31, 2016, a passively managed portfolio with 60 percent stocks (a S&P 500 ETF) and 40 percent bonds (the Barclays Aggregate ETF) had an annualized return of 6.7 percent with a standard deviation of 9.4 percent, a Sharpe ratio of 0.66, and maximum one-year drawdown of 27.7 percent.[3]

Now, for contrast, let's look at a portfolio that incorporates both traditional and alternative asset classes: This portfolio comprises 40 percent stocks (S&P 500 ETF), 30 percent bonds (Barclays Aggregate ETF), 5 percent real estate (Dow Jones REIT Index), 5 percent commodities (Morningstar U.S. Commodities Index), 10 percent managed futures (Credit Suisse Managed Futures Index), and 10 percent market-neutral long/short

(CIDSM Market Neutral Index). According to Morningstar, over the same 10-year period, the more diversified portfolio had a 6.4 percent return, a standard deviation of 7.9 percent, a Sharpe ratio of 0.74, and maximum one-year drawdown of 22.1 percent.[4]

The portfolio containing alternative assets sacrificed some return, but showed superior risk-adjusted return metrics. As we have discussed in depth, higher-net-worth investors need to focus on risk-adjusted returns and, more important, on minimizing volatility and downside drawdown. This portfolio achieved that goal as it delivered 95 percent of the return, with 85 percent of the volatility, and 80 percent of the downside drawdown.

Higher-net-worth investors should think of alternatives in two ways: either as a return enhancer or as a portfolio diversifier. The portfolio analysis shows the powerful benefits of non-correlated assets as diversifiers. In my opinion, that is the single most important benefit of incorporating alternative strategies for the higher-net-worth investor.

However, it's inadvisable to ignore return enhancement, as both can be beneficial to long-term wealth creation. If the traditional portfolio had incorporated the proper mix of return enhancers, not only the risk metrics but also absolute returns would be more favorable. Higher-net-worth investors simply need to be cognizant of what they are investing in and what the net effect is on risk. For example, publicly traded REITs can offer both return enhancement and diversification benefits, but during times of stress, publicly traded REITs will fall with the rest of the stock market—a correlation of 1.0.

For this reason, a private real estate investment that is less correlated to stock market–specific performance might be more appropriate for higher-net-worth individuals. Through June 30, 2016, private equity (as measured by the Global Buyout and Growth Equity Index) had a 20-year annualized return of 13 percent. This trounces public equity markets, whereas the correlation to the S&P 500 is close to 0.8. This is a return enhancer you should consider as a replacement for a portion of your traditional equity exposure, not simply as a tool to minimize volatility.

NOT ABOUT BIG BETS AND HOME RUNS

The biggest issue with high-net-worth investors is that they focus on return enhancers and fall in love with the big-name managers who make massive bets. Many of the well-known hedge fund managers become famous due to one big trade or period of performance. They then attract large amounts of capital and start taking concentrated bets on specific companies, which can lead to outsized returns. This can be a great strategy, but remember, the manager is compensated based on a management fee and a percentage of the upside. Given human nature, this can lead to inappropriate risk taking.

The purpose of hedged strategies is exactly that—to *hedge* market risk. That's what makes them uncorrelated assets. There are many hedge fund managers—and even publicly traded long/short funds—with proven, systematic processes for increasing diversification, neutralizing beta, and achieving superior risk-adjusted returns. Consulting with an advisor who fully understands these methods and can evaluate risk/reward metrics over multiple periods is the best way to determine the net benefit of these complex investments.

Investing in private investments and publicly traded, hedged strategies has proven to enhance risk-adjusted returns. These strategies should be a component of any higher-net-worth investor's portfolio. But such investors must be cognizant of what they own and must understand each asset's role in the overall portfolio. Additionally, it's important that no more than 10 percent of your assets be in a single strategy. This promotes increased diversification and risk-management benefits. This is where a financial advisor who understands the complexities of this market and can offer exposure at reasonable minimum investment levels becomes highly beneficial.

Crossing the Wealth Line

» *If you're an Affluent or MCM investor who's new to alternative investments, market-neutral strategies are a great place to start. By design, they do not correlate with the market.*

» *Consider using an ETF or a mutual fund version, which would be available at lower investment minimums.*

KEY #9:

TAX SAVINGS ADD UP

Science says that the human brain is the most complex construct in the universe. Many finance professionals would disagree. Instead, the universe has reserved its greatest complexity for the United States Tax Code. It's byzantine, counterintuitive, and impossible to understand without years of study. That's why higher-net-worth investors need assistance to use it to their advantage.

Some people, however, do succeed in offering relatively simple explanations of how our progressive taxation system works. One of the cleverest turns up online every so often, as on the *International Liberty* blog:[1]

> Suppose that every day, 10 men go out for beer and the bill for all 10 comes to $100. If they paid their bill the way we pay our taxes, it would go something like this...
>
> » The first four men (the poorest) would pay nothing.

» The fifth would pay $1.

» The sixth would pay $3.

» The seventh would pay $7.

» The eighth would pay $12.

» The ninth would pay $18.

» The tenth man (the richest) would pay $59.

So, that's what they decided to do. The 10 men drank in the bar every day and seemed quite happy with the arrangement, until one day, the owner threw them a curve ball.

"Since you are all such good customers," he said, "I'm going to reduce the cost of your daily beer by $20." Drinks for the 10 men would now cost just $80.

The group still wanted to pay their bill the way we pay our taxes. So the first four men were unaffected. They would still drink for free. But what about the other six? How could they divide the $20 windfall so that everyone would get his fair share?

The bar owner suggested that it would be fair to reduce each man's bill by a higher percentage the poorer he was, to follow the principle of the tax system they had been using, and he proceeded to work out the amounts he suggested that each should now pay:

» And so the fifth man, like the first four, now paid nothing (100% savings).

> » The sixth now paid $2 instead of $3 (33% savings).

> » The seventh now paid $5 instead of $7 (28% savings).

> » The eighth now paid $9 instead of $12 (25% savings).

> » The ninth now paid $14 instead of $18 (22% savings).

> » The tenth now paid $49 instead of $59 (16% savings).

Each of the six was better off than before. And the first four continued to drink for free. But once outside the bar, the men began to compare their savings.

"I only got a dollar out of the $20 savings," declared the sixth man. He pointed to the tenth man, the richest. "But he got $10!"

"Yeah, that's right," exclaimed the fifth man. "I only saved a dollar, too. It's unfair that he got 10 times the benefit I got!"

"That's true!" shouted the seventh man. "Why should he get $10 back, when I got only $2? The wealthy get all the breaks!"

"Wait a minute," yelled the first four men in unison, "we didn't get anything at all. This new tax system exploits the poor!"

The nine men surrounded the tenth and beat him up.

The next night the tenth man didn't show up for drinks. The nine sat down and had their beers without him. But when it came time to pay the bill, they discovered something important: They didn't have enough money between all of them for even half of the bill!

In our tax system, the wealthier you are, the more you pay, and the more the system depends on your tax revenues to provide services for others. But it doesn't always work out that way in practice. For instance, in 2011, Buffett wrote an editorial in *The New York Times* titled "Stop Coddling the Super-Rich," where he claimed that his taxes amounted to only 17.4 percent of his taxable income. PolitiFact checked the story during the 2016 presidential campaign and confirmed that it's true. How? Buffett's income comes primarily through investments, which are taxed at the capital gains rate, lower than the marginal tax rate at which his assistant's wages are taxed.

Bottom line: How much you pay—or don't pay—varies depending on many factors. If you want to minimize your tax burden within the tax laws, you can't go it alone.

THE POWER OF TAX MANAGEMENT

Taxation has a powerful effect on your ability to accumulate long-term wealth, and proper tax management can have a greater positive impact on both your income and the net returns on your investments than any other advice your wealth management team can provide. It's laudable to believe in paying your fair share of taxes as a citizen of the United States; you should absolutely pay your legal tax obligation. However, what determines your fair share? The tax laws as written are filled with opportunities for wealthy investors to reduce their tax burden

100 percent legally, so shouldn't you take advantage? Paying your taxes is patriotic; paying more than you have to is foolish and costly.

Of course, the tax code is also mind-numbingly complex. To find every permissible means of reducing the taxes you owe, you need the assistance of not only a good financial advisor but a terrific CPA and tax attorney.

Taxation affects your wealth in two main ways. First, after you pay taxes, you have less money to invest. Obviously, if you're investing $100,000 instead of $200,000, you're not going to earn as much. Having less to invest could even shut you out of certain investments, such as hedge funds. Over time, that can really eat away at your returns. One way around this is to use tax-advantaged accounts like traditional IRAs and 401(k)s. Because your taxable income is reduced by the amount you deposit in those accounts, you're effectively investing your income *before* you pay taxes on it.

That's useful for the Middle-Class Millionaire, who is primarily investing in a tax-deferred environment. But what about for higher-net-worth investors with substantial holdings in taxable accounts?

The second way taxes impact your wealth is, of course, that they reduce your real returns—what's left after you pay taxes on your gains. No matter what or how you invest, if your investments increase in value, eventually you will have to pay taxes on those gains. Even investing in tax-deferred accounts like 401(k)s spares you from taxes only temporarily; when you retire and start withdrawing money from those accounts, you have to pay income tax on it.

How much can taxes impact your returns on your investments? One example uses two hypothetical 40-year investments, both with annual $4,000 contributions and earning 8 percent per year. The difference: One is a 401(k) account, and one is a taxable account subject to annual capital gains tax. After 40 years, the tax-deferred 401(k) was worth $103,000 more than the taxable account—even after the deferred taxes were paid on the 401(k) assets.

A more concise example comes from Andy Rachleff, co-founder and executive chairman of Wealthfront. He writes that an investor using effective strategies to minimize taxes and be more tax efficient could save more than 3 percent annually on taxes. That might not sound like much, but for a higher-net-worth investor with several million dollars in assets, mostly in nonqualified accounts, over 30 years that 3 percent could equal hundreds of thousands of dollars in savings.

A REVIEW OF HOW TAXES WORK

Before you can appreciate how tax minimization and efficiency strategies can benefit you, it's important that you understand how the different kinds of taxes work and affect your portfolio. Perhaps this is already familiar to you. Even so, there are so many misconceptions about taxes that it's vital to get some clarity.

Three types of taxes are of concern to higher-net-worth investors:

1. **Income taxes.** Income taxes are subject to the *marginal tax rate*, the system you're probably familiar with that separates people into tax brackets based on income. What makes marginal tax rates unique is that as your income rises, you're taxed at a higher tax rate on that income. So your tax bracket is actually the amount of tax you pay on your highest dollar of taxable income. As you probably also know, in addition to federal income tax, most states levy a state income tax. Many cities also levy a city income or flat earnings tax. This tax system is confusing to many people. It's important to understand that as you move into a higher tax bracket, you will not be taxed at that higher rate retroactive to your first dollar of income. Rather, you'll be taxed at that new higher rate only on the incremental earnings in that bracket.

2. **Capital gains tax.** This is the tax that is most relevant to wealthy investors. Capital gains tax is the tax you pay on the appreciation of an asset—a stock, a piece of real estate, a collectible—when you sell it. If you sell something for more than your *basis*—the amount you paid for it—then you owe tax on that difference. Capital gains tax rates vary by your tax bracket and often fluctuate over time, but today they range from zero to 20 percent (although most higher-net-worth investors will be in the 15 to 20 percent range) if they're considered long-term, or as high as 39.6 percent

if considered short-term. For you, as a higher-net-worth individual, capital gains taxes will probably be the most relevant tax, so you should know a few critical things about it. First, you pay capital gains taxes only when you sell an asset. As long as you hold the asset without selling it, you're not *realizing* a financial gain, so there is no taxable event. Remember the earlier discussion about the risk of having a surprise taxable event if a stock within a mutual fund that you own was sold after appreciating? That's capital gains tax. Second, the length of time you hold an asset matters. The capital gains tax rates are very different if you sell an asset after owning it for less than one year versus selling after more than a year. If you sell after less than a year, your capital gains tax rate is the same as your marginal income tax rate. So if you're in the 39.6 percent bracket, you're paying 39.6 percent federal capital gains tax. But if you sell after one year, your rate drops to 20 percent. Let's assume you're in the highest tax bracket, you purchased stock for $500,000, and five years later you sold it for $1 million—a nice $500,000 capital gain. Because you held that stock for more than a year, you would net $900,000 from that sale (after paying $100,000 in tax). But suppose that instead, you bought those shares at the company's IPO and they skyrocketed to double your purchase price in nine months. If you decided to take your profits and sell before a year had elapsed, you would net $802,000—$98,000 less—because your capital gains tax rate would be almost 20 points higher. The last thing to know is that capital losses can offset your capital gains. Inevitably, some investments lose value; that's the nature of markets. However, you can apply losses against your gains to reduce your capital gains tax burden, and you can carry some losses forward into future tax years to reduce your tax liability.

3. **Medicare tax.** The net investment income tax (NIIT) went into effect in 2013. It imposes a 3.8 percent tax on the investment income of individuals, estates, and trusts that reach specific income levels. If you're single with a modified adjusted gross income, or MAGI, of more than $200,000, or if you're married with a MAGI of more than $250,000, you will have to pay this tax on interest, dividends, capital gains, and royalty income from things like selling stocks, rent on rental properties, and the sale of real estate.[2]

MARGINAL VERSUS EFFECTIVE TAX RATE

There. That's all you need to know about taxes, right? Not really. There's a reason the U.S. Tax Code runs nearly 75,000 pages. No, that's not a misprint. Taxation is unbelievably complex, which is why top tax attorneys go to school for two additional years to earn a master of laws in taxation. To simplify things, let's talk about what's relevant for you: *marginal* tax rates versus *effective* tax rates, and which matters more for the higher-net-worth investor.

As explained earlier, the marginal tax rate is what you think of as your tax bracket. Here are the details about the marginal federal tax brackets along with the long-term capital gains tax rates:

However, as mentioned earlier, your marginal tax rate is not the same as the amount of tax you pay. A marginal tax rate of 39.6 percent doesn't mean you're going to send nearly 40 percent of your income to Uncle Sam every year. The way our tax system works, the marginal tax rate at each level applies only to the taxable income you earn above that threshold. So if your taxable income is $500,000 and you're filing jointly, you're going to pay that 39.6 top rate on only $29,300 of that income—the amount over the $470,700 line.

Make sense? Let's make it even clearer by breaking down exactly how much that couple with a $500,000 taxable income would pay in federal taxes:

Income	You would pay . . .
$0–$18,650	$1,865
$18,651–$75,900	$8,587.50
$75,901–$153,100	$19,300
$153,101–$233,350	$22,470
$233,350–$416,700	$60,505.50
$416,701–$470,700	$18,900
$470,701–$500,000	$11,602
TOTAL TAX OWED	$143,230

Based on these numbers, you would owe the IRS approximately 28.7 percent of your taxable income. That's your *effective tax rate*. State taxes work according to the same bracket system, so strategies that work to reduce your federal tax debt also work to reduce your state tax debt (unless you live in a state with no income tax, in which case it's not an issue).

In the end, our goal is to bring down your effective tax rate—the dollars you actually send to Uncle Sam—and leave more money in your pocket. Because of the way federal taxes are calculated, however, financial advisors achieve this goal by using strategies that reduce your tax liability at your marginal tax rate. In the end, it's your marginal rate that really matters.

HOW A FINANCIAL ADVISOR CAN REDUCE YOUR TAXES

Savvy financial advisors will address their tax planning toward your highest tax bracket. By doing this, they can slide your taxable income up or down based on the last dollars you've earned. So if you're in that top 39.6 percent federal bracket, a quality tax strategy will focus on saving you money at that top level.

Let's take our hypothetical couple with $500,000 in taxable income paying the 39.6 percent marginal tax rate. If their advisor implemented a tax strategy that reduced their taxable income by $20,000, that would save them $7,920 in taxes ($20,000 x 39.6 percent) and drop their federal tax debt to around $135,000—an effective tax rate of 27 percent. That's important, because they're saving approximately $8,000, not $5,400 ($20,000 x 27 percent). That illustrates why it's the marginal tax rate, not the effective tax rate, that matters in tax planning.

Tax planning isn't as important for lower-income investors because the bulk of their investments are in tax-advantaged accounts. But for higher-net-worth investors, whose portfolios are throwing off income regularly, tax minimization strategies that bring tax liability down by a few percentage points can potentially make a difference of thousands or tens of thousands of dollars. That's more money back in your pocket to reinvest or to fund the lifestyle you enjoy. Now, let's look at some of the strategies used to save investors on their taxes.

TAX MINIMIZATION STRATEGIES

There are many tax minimization tools available to higher-net-worth investors:

» **Exchange funds.** An investor buys shares in a single stock for $200,000 and watches it appreciate to $1 million. That's fantastic—except that it comes with a potentially huge capital gains tax bill. Plus, being that heavily invested in a single stock increases the investor's risk. It's in the investor's best interest to diversify, but selling the stock means getting hit with more than $160,000 in taxes. Instead, a product offered by large brokerage firms will transfer the $1 million

2017 Federal Income Tax Rates - on Taxable Income

(Parenthesis after bracket indiciates base tax amount plus percentage on amount over lower limit for that bracket)

Marginal Rate	Single ($)	Married Filing Jointly (MFJ)	Head of House-hold (HoH)	Married Filing Separately (MFS)	Estates and Trusts	Long Term Capital Gains**	Qualified Dividends**
10%	$0 - $9,325	$0 - $18,650	$0 - $13,350	$0 - $9,325	n/a	0%	0%
15%	$9,325 - $37,950 ($932.50 + 15%)	$18,560 - $75,900 ($1,865 + 15%)	$13,350 - $50,800 ($1,335 + 15%)	$9,325 - $37,950 ($932.50 +15%)	$0 -2,550 ($0 + 15%)	0%	0%
25%	$37,950 - $91,900 ($5,226.25 + 25%)	$75,900 - $153,100 ($10,452.50 + 25%)	$50,800 - $131,200 ($6,952.50 + 25%)	$37,950 - $76,550 ($5,226.25 + 25%)	$2,550 - $6,000 ($382.50 + 25%)	15%	15%
28%	$91,900 - $191,650 ($18,713.75 + 28%)	$153,100 - $233,350 ($29,752.50 + 28%)	$131,200 - $212,500 ($27,052.50 + 28%)	$76,550 - $116,675 ($14,876.25 + 28%)	$6,000 - $9,150 ($1,245 + 28%)	15%	15%
33%	$191,650 -$416,700 ($46,643.75 + 33%)	$233,350 - $416,700 ($52,222.50 + 33%)	$212,500 - $416,700 ($49,816.50 + 33%)	$116,675 - $208,350 ($26,111.25 + 33%)	$9,150 - $12,500 ($2,127 + 33%)	15%*	15%*
35%	$416,700 - $418,400 ($120,910.25 + 35%)	$416,700 - $470,700 ($112,728 + 35%)	$416,700 - $444,500 ($117,202.50 + 35%)	$208,350 - $235,350 ($56,364 + 35%)	n/a	15%*	15%*
39.6%	$418,400 and up ($121,505.25 + 39.6%)	$470,700 and up ($131,628 + 39.6%)	$444,500 and up ($126,950 + 39.6%)	$235,350 and up ($65,814 + 39.6%)	$12,500 and up ($3,232.50 + 39.6%)	20%*	20%*

* 3.8% Medicare tax on investment income will also be imposed for single taxpayers with MAGI above $200,000 and married filing jointly with MAGI > $250,000 (MFS > $125,000)

** Short term capital gains (investments held less than one year) and non-qualified dividends are taxed at your marginal income tax rate in stock into an exchange fund that pools our investor's assets with those of other investors who also have concentrated positions. Our investor would now own shares in this new fund. This would not be a taxable event, and it would dramatically increase the investor's diversification, adjusting overall risk downward. The alpha—the investor's risk-adjusted return—would be higher, and the ride would be smoother. Remember, at the higher-net-worth level, a smooth ride is everything.

» **Options collar.** Let's say that same investor has $1 million in stock and doesn't want to do an exchange fund transfer. Our investor really likes the stock and the company. Instead, the investor could use an options collar strategy to help protect his or her position and stay in that stock with lower risk. The higher-net-worth investor sells an out-of-the-money "call" option. This means if the buyer of the call chooses to exercise the option, the investor is obligated to sell the stock to that buyer at a designated price or "strike." This price is said to be out of the money because the strike is above the current price. This limits the upside that the higher-net-worth investor can experience on the stock, but the buyer has to pay him or her a premium to gain this right. In turn, our investor uses that premium to buy an out-of-the-money "put" contract on the stock. This gives the investor the right, not the obligation, to sell at a designated price within a certain time period. The contract is said to be out of the money because the strike price is below the current price. Basically, the financial advisor has put a collar around the position so that the price won't rise above or fall below a certain level. The beauty of options contracts is that their value adjusts according to the current price of the stock and can be bought and sold. This prevents any forced sale of the stock that would trigger capital gains.

» **Tax loss harvesting.** An earlier chapter cited a Vanguard white paper that details the various ways in which a financial advisor adds bottom-line value to an investor's portfolio, including the value of managing investor behavior. Well, another point of added value comes from tax loss harvesting. Tax loss harvesting is selling assets that have lost value, and locking in your losses in order to reduce or even eliminate the capital gains taxes on other assets that have increased in value. With a long-term capital gains tax rate of 20 percent for wealthy investors, plus the 3.8 percent Medicare surtax (NIIT), that can be pretty useful.

Here is an example: Bill is in the 33 percent marginal tax bracket, and two years ago he bought $200,000 in Very Big Corporation stock. That stock has lost value over the past two years and is now worth $190,000. Bill decides to sell the stock and lock in a loss of $10,000 in order to tax loss harvest. He can use that loss to offset capital gains on other investments, reducing his net capital gain. So if he made $25,000 selling another stock, he could apply his $10,000 loss and reduce his net capital gain to $15,000. If his capital losses exceed his capital gains for the year, he can use up to $3,000 of his loss to offset ordinary income, saving himself $1,000 in taxes ($3,000 x 33 percent). He can take the unused $7,000 of his capital loss and carry it forward to future tax years to offset future gains.

Doing this can take some convincing for some investors. Because of the disposition effect (described earlier), investors don't like the idea of locking in losses. But the potential benefits are very real. Tax loss harvesting has been shown to add 35 to 75 basis points annually to investors' real returns. If you have a $10 million portfolio of taxable assets, 50 extra basis points is an extra $50,000 in your pocket. Would you rather give that money to the U.S. Treasury or use it to send your child to the Ivy League?

There are some other limitations beyond the $3,000 annual cap on income offsets. The most notable is the "wash rule." This piece of the tax code says that you can't take a capital loss on a security if you rebuy that same security or buy something substantially identical 30 days before or after you sell. (When you include the day that you sell the depreciated security, the wash rule applies throughout a 61-day window.) Individual stocks are not considered identical, so the rule doesn't apply to them, but selling one S&P 500 index fund one day and buying another S&P index fund the next day would be a violation.

Let's say you're in Home Depot stock, and it happens to be down that year. You don't love the company, but you like stocks in the home improvement sector. You could sell your

Home Depot stock at the end of the year for a $50,000 loss, use it to reduce your income for the year, and buy stock in Lowe's. You'd still have a position in the home improvement industry, just through another company. But if you tried to do the same thing with two S&P 500 index funds, the IRS would disallow your claimed loss. This rule also prevents you from selling a security and turning around and buying it inside your IRA within the 61-day window. Tax loss harvesting comes with a lot of caveats and restrictions, which is a good reason to rely on your advisor.

» **Asset location.** Holding different assets in some tax-qualified environments such as IRAs or 401(k)s can reduce or defer your taxes on those assets. The benefit comes from how different forms of income are taxed. Interest income is taxed at the marginal income tax rate, while long-term capital gains and qualified dividends are taxed at the lower capital gains rate. So it's advantageous for investors to have equity investments like stocks, which generate returns from appreciation and dividends, in taxable accounts, where they will be subject to the lower capital gains tax rate, instead of holding them in tax-deferred retirement accounts like IRAs, where monies withdrawn would be subject to the much higher marginal income tax rate.

It's also beneficial to hold more growth-oriented investments in taxable accounts because if they lose value, those losses can be more easily harvested to offset capital gains. Meanwhile, investments that throw off regular income, such as taxable bonds and mutual funds that pay annual distributions, are better held in tax-advantaged accounts, allowing those taxes to be deferred for years. Additionally, high-turnover strategies should be held in tax-advantaged accounts to avoid excessive realized short-term and long-term capital gains that may increase your tax obligation due to fund manager activity that's outside of your control.

Asset location is not an exact science. A lot of it depends on the ratio of dollars you have available in taxable versus tax-advantaged accounts. Your advisor and your financial team will help you determine which of your assets should be held in what kind of accounts based on your unique situation.

» **Net unrealized appreciation (NUA).** If you work for a company and have company stock in your 401(k), any money you withdraw from that 401(k) is taxed at the marginal rate. However, if the company stock has appreciated, NUA offers a way to make sure that at least part of that stock is taxed at the more favorable capital gains rate. This is how it works: When you request a distribution of the company stock in your 401(k), you have it deposited in a taxable account, such as a brokerage account. You will pay taxes on the stock at the marginal income tax rate, but only on the cost basis of the stock—the average price of the shares when they were contributed to your 401(k). The key is that you don't have to pay taxes on the appreciation of the company stock until you sell it, and the proceeds of that sale are taxed at the long-term capital gains rate . . . even if you have held the stock for less than one year.

» **Master limited partnership (MLP).** These are often tied to the energy industry, which means they can be highly volatile as energy prices rise and fall. However, MLPs offer hefty distributions that may be mostly tax-free due to depreciation. This depreciation does reduce your cost basis, meaning you could have a higher income-tax bill if the assets were sold.

Here is an example: If you were to invest $100,000 in an MLP, your cost basis (the taxable value of the investment) is $100,000. However, every time a distribution is paid, the amount of the distribution that isn't taxable reduces your basis. Assuming you received a 5 percent distribution, it would reduce your basis by 5 percent each year.

This makes MLPs a great vehicle for transferring wealth. Let's say the $100,000 stock you've owned for 10 years is now worth $200,000, and you have received $50,000 of tax-free distributions. This means your cost basis is now $50,000 ($100,000 minus $50,000), and your long-term capital gain would be $150,000 if you sold. But let's say you want to pass that wealth to your children, so you hold the stock for 10 more years, each of which pays a 5 percent distribution. With some appreciation, the stock's total value is now $300,000, but 20 years of distributions have reduced your basis to below zero. At your death, the stock would transfer to your beneficiaries, and they would get a step-up in basis to the $300,000 full market value of the stock. Your children could then sell that stock at its full $300,000 value with no capital gains tax.

» **No-load variable annuities.** A variable annuity is a tax-deferred retirement account that lets you put your money in a variety of investments that you select, and then pays you retirement income based on the performance of those investments. However, "loaded" variable annuities often involve substantial fees, commissions, and surrender charges. Often they are actively managed with high turnover, creating an excess of taxable events for the investor. Such annuities have no place in a higher-net-worth individual's investment strategy.

"No-load" variable annuities have low or no fees or surrender charges, so your money can be withdrawn without paying the penalty commonly levied against account holders for early cancellation of an annuity or insurance contract. They also place your strategy in a tax-advantaged wrapper. This could be beneficial for those high-turnover, active management strategies that would normally trigger hefty tax bills in a taxable account.

» **ESOP 1042 rollover.** If you own a business, you have the potential to defer capital gains tax if you sell your business (or shares of your business) to an employee stock ownership plan, or ESOP. If you have held the company stock for at least three years, the ESOP owns at least 30 percent of the total stock after the sale. And if you reinvest the proceeds of the stock sale into a qualified replacement property, or QRP (usually, a publicly traded security), within one year of the ESOP sale, you may either defer capital gains taxes or, if you pass the QRP to your estate, avoid them completely.

Needless to say, these tax minimization strategies—and this is only a partial list—are complex and fraught with pitfalls for even the most experienced investors. What you should know is that there are many proven strategies available to mitigate your potential tax liability. Be sure to consult with your financial advisor, tax attorney, and accountant to determine which strategies fit best with your portfolio and goals in order to enjoy the greatest possible tax savings.

Crossing the Wealth Line

» *If you're starting to place more assets in taxable investments, you're probably also interested in minimizing taxes on those investments. Begin by working with your advisor to optimize your asset location. Make sure you have the right investments in the most efficient places: Roth IRAs, traditional IRAs, other kinds of qualified accounts, taxable accounts.*

» *Once you've done this, consider the benefits of a Roth conversion. There are many strategies for using Roth conversions to your advantage.*

THE SOONER, THE BETTER WHEN IT COMES TO ESTATE PLANNING

Estate planning is like life insurance: It's something that a lot of people don't like to think about because it reminds them of their mortality. Well, refusing to talk about death doesn't make it go away. There's a really good reason to have a conversation with your professional team about your estate plan, even if you're only 40 and healthy as a horse: It can benefit you financially while you're still on this side of the grass.

Estate planning is a critical element of financial planning that too many investors overlook. According to legal services company

Rocket Lawyer, as of 2014 about 50 percent of Americans ages 55 to 64 don't have any sort of estate plan—not even a will. A basic will is essential, because if you die without one (a circumstance the legal system calls "intestate"), state laws carried out in probate court, not you, will decide what happens to your assets. This can saddle your heirs with a nasty legal bill in addition to a tax burden. Everyone should have some sort of estate plan, regardless of their income.

For higher-net-worth investors, estate planning is even more important—not only because you have more assets to pass on to your beneficiaries, but because you'd like to optimize the wealth that you've accumulated. You may have a business that you want your children to inherit. You may be helping support multiple charitable organizations or be a major contributor to your alma mater's endowment. Most of all, you want to make sure your spouse, kids, grandchildren, and other family members are taken care of should something happen to you—without leaving them with a huge tax burden along the way. And by the way, Uncle Sam is not really part of your family. You need to disinherit him!

Proper estate and gift planning benefits you in numerous ways:

» Ensures that your wealth goes to the people and causes you care about in a timely and efficient manner, not into the coffers of government bureaucrats

» Helps ensure that your wishes are followed in case you are incapacitated, especially if you have a living trust, living will, or power of attorney

» Provides your heirs with sufficient cash to cover taxes and expenses without being forced to sell assets, which can depress the value of those assets *and* create taxable events (especially when you hold highly illiquid assets like a privately owned business or real estate)

» Allows you to continue supporting the charities that are most important to you

» Allows you to transfer wealth to your children and grandchildren through tax-free gifts while you're still around to enjoy their gratitude

» Helps avoid misunderstandings and bad feelings when heirs are confused about who gets what or the validity of a will

Finally, estate planning can help you determine your legacy—what you leave behind when you're gone. If you've worked as hard as some people do to build your wealth, you're proud of what you've done and you want to leave your mark on the world. Whatever that means to you, an estate plan can help you do it.

In the end, leaving estate planning to chance is virtually guaranteed to cause headaches and heartaches for your beneficiaries, and might even damage your legacy. Remember actor Heath Ledger, who won the Academy Award for his portrayal of the Joker in *The Dark Knight*? You probably also remember that he died tragically of a prescription drug overdose in 2008. But after his death, it was discovered that his will had not been updated since 2003, so neither his partner, Michelle Williams, nor their daughter, Matilda Rose, had been included in his will. As a result, everything went to Ledger's parents and sisters, causing a family rift at a time of pain.

Or there's the case of former Miami Dolphins owner Joe Robbie. Before he passed away in 1990, he established a trust whose primary asset was two partnerships that together owned an 88 percent stake in the Dolphins. His intention was to pass majority ownership in the team to his heirs and keep the team in the family. But the trust left the family liable for $47 million in estate taxes, and Robbie's heirs were forced to sell a 50 percent interest in the team and a stake in Joe Robbie Stadium to Blockbuster Video magnate Wayne Huizenga in order to pay the tax debt. So a lack of proper planning wound up cancelling out Robbie's best intentions.

More recently, we have music legend Prince, who died in 2016. He died without a will, which means that his financial affairs have become a matter of public record. Now Prince's sister and five half-siblings, as well as other people who claim to be family members, are fighting over the spoils. Nobody is even sure of the value of his estate. So the legacy of a great artist is tarnished by squabbling when he's no longer around to defend it.

Don't leave the fate of your estate to chance. Now is the time to plan.

THE BASICS

But first, what is an estate? Your estate consists of all assets that are in your name or partially in your name, including your home and other real estate, your car, your bank accounts, your investments, and even intellectual property such as inventions or books you've published. It also includes (and this is the part that people often forget) any debts you owe when you die. So if you leave your house to your grandson and he becomes the sole owner, it will fall to him to pay any outstanding mortgage balance.

For a long time, the laws around estate planning, estate taxes, and gift taxes seemed to change from year to year. The estate tax even disappeared completely in 2010, only to stage a comeback the following year. This made long-term estate planning extremely challenging for those of us in the wealth management business. But we seem to have settled into a steady state in the past few years, and while that can be subject to change depending on the political climate, the advice in this book assumes that things will stay the way they are for a while.

If you have an estate worth anything up to approximately $5.5 million, then you don't even need to worry about federal estate taxes, because the federal government has a $5.49 million (for 2017) per-person estate tax exemption. That means you and your spouse can pass up to roughly $11 million to future generations, free of estate tax. Only about 0.3 percent of taxpayers are estimated to have estates large enough to incur the tax, so it might not even be an issue for you today. However, if you're already in a higher-net-worth category—or if you have 20 or 30 years of investing ahead of you, during which your wealth is likely to increase—estate taxes are very relevant.

Any part of your estate valued beyond the individual or joint limits is taxed at a federal rate ranging from 18 percent to 40 percent. This handy table illustrates how federal estate taxes impact the first $1 million over the exemption:

Lower Limit	Upper Limit	Initial Taxation	Further Taxation
0	$10,000	$0	18% of the amount
$10,000	$20,000	$1,800	20% of the excess
$20,000	$40,000	$3,800	22% of the excess
$40,000	$60,000	$8,200	24% of the excess
$60,000	$80,000	$13,000	26% of the excess
$80,000	$100,000	$18,000	28% of the excess
$100,000	$150,000	$23,000	30% of the excess
$150,000	$250,000	$38,000	32% of the excess
$250,000	$500,000	$70,800	34% of the excess
$500,000	$750,000	$155,800	37% of the excess
$750,000	$1,000,000	$248,300	39% of the excess
$1,000,000	and over	$345,800	40% of the excess

In addition, 15 states and the District of Columbia have their own estate taxes, six states have an inheritance tax, and Maryland and New Jersey have both (yikes). State-specific exemption levels (typically much lower) and tax rates vary widely, so check with your professional team about your overall state estate tax exposure. (Incidentally, a lack of estate tax concerns doesn't mean you have no need for an estate plan. You still need a plan to determine the distribution of your assets to your beneficiaries.)

What goes into an estate plan? Apart from the financial planning, there are some essential documents that can make up a plan:

» **Last will and testament.** This is the must-have component of any estate plan. A will lets you decide who inherits your assets, designate guardians for your minor children, and choose the executor—the person responsible for ensuring that your wishes are carried out and all necessary final tax returns are filed. Your will is the only vehicle that lets you make these decisions.

» **Living will.** A living will is not about the afterlife, but the end of life. It lets you designate and decide what care you want if you are incapacitated or hospitalized and can't speak for yourself. For example, if you do not want to be resuscitated after going into cardiac arrest, you can place a Do Not Resuscitate order in your living will.

» **Revocable trust.** Also called a "living trust," this instrument lets you assign your assets to people or nonprofit organizations such as charities or schools. This tool can help your assets pass outside of probate, while maintaining control of the assets during your lifetime.

» **Power of attorney (POA).** This document empowers a responsible individual to make decisions on your behalf when you are unable to do so yourself. A *durable* power of attorney designates someone as your trusted agent to make financial decisions regarding your estate. This person may not overrule the terms of your will or trust, but can do things like make investment decisions or enter into real estate transactions on your behalf. A *healthcare* power of attorney assigns someone to make healthcare decisions for you, presumably based on knowing your wishes regarding lifesaving measures and so on. You choose to grant POA to competent individuals whom you trust, such as financially experienced family members or your longtime lawyer.

Beyond those essential legal instruments, any estate plan has to answer some bigger questions. Do you want to keep the details of your finances private? Do you want to pass along a business to your heirs? Do you want to help your family avoid unnecessary taxation? Are there charitable organizations you would like to support?

Estate planning offers you ways to freeze the value of your estate so that your assets experience as much of their future appreciation as possible outside of your taxable estate. By doing that, you can minimize or even eliminate much of the estate tax burden on your heirs. Let's review some of the ways you can make that happen.

GIFTING

You're allowed to give each of your heirs—children, grandchildren, sons- or daughters-in-law—up to $14,000 (for 2017) each per year, completely tax-free. This annual gift exclusion is allowed for family members and anyone else, including friends, neighbors, and such. As long as you don't exceed that annual limit, the recipients don't have to pay income tax on the money; nor do you or your beneficiaries have to pay gift tax or file a gift tax return. Note that for married couples, each spouse can give $14,000. That's extremely useful if you want to gradually pass along wealth to your heirs, year after year, without also passing on a tax debt. So if you have three children, over 10 years you and your spouse could give them a total of $840,000 ([$28,000 x 3] x 10) without anyone paying a dime in tax.

Anything over $14,000 not only triggers the need to file a federal gift tax return (Form 709), but also eats away at your estate tax exemption. (Note: You don't owe gift tax until you've exceeded the annual gifting exclusion and you've eaten up all of the exemption, roughly $5.5 million per person exemption.)

For example, let's say your granddaughter turns 18 and is accepted to Harvard. For each of the next four years, you give her $30,000 to help pay her tuition. That's very generous, but it has a downside: A gift over the $14,000 limit (or $28,000 for a couple) requires the giver to file a gift tax return. You don't have to pay any taxes on your gift, but you do reduce your estate tax exemption by $64,000 ($30,000–$14,000 = $16,000 x 4 = $64,000). That means your heirs will have to pay estate taxes on the portion of your estate that remains above that newly reduced exemption amount.

The federal gift tax law has two loopholes that, if used properly, can allow you to pay for education and medical bills without the need for a gift tax return and without reducing your annual exclusion amount for the person who benefits from your payment. If you pay tuition (for anyone) or pay medical bills (for anyone) and you write the check directly to the school or hospital, it does not count as a gift.

Think of that lifetime estate tax exemption as a well that you draw from. As long as you stay at the annual exclusion or below it, the well will replenish itself. Gift more than the limit, and you slowly deplete the well. If your eventual estate is unlikely to be near $5.5 million, this doesn't matter much from a federal estate tax perspective. But if it is likely to be large enough to incur estate taxes, you need to plan your gifts with more care.

GIFTING A BUSINESS

One of the most common ways that parents gift value to their children is by passing on a business. Well, any business you give to your heirs is going to exceed the $14,000 gift limit. So how do you reduce the impact on your estate tax exemption? One way is through gifting valuation discounts. Proposed regulations under Section 2704 of the Internal Revenue Code could significantly restrict valuation discount planning for family-controlled businesses in regards to estate taxes, gifts, and generation-skipping transfers. Talk to your advisor to stay current on this possible change and its impact on your financial strategy.

Let's assume you own 100 percent of a business worth $10 million, and you wish to start gifting that business to your child while you're alive. If you give your child 1 percent of that business per year for 10 years, that's $100,000 per year or a total of $1 million. Obviously, that's way over the annual gift tax exclusion. Even if you and your spouse each gift $14,000 per year, that's only $28,000, leaving $72,000 per year eating away at the estate tax exemption. Over 10 years, you would reduce the amount of your estate that's exempt from estate taxes by $720,000. So what do you do?

Instead of simply giving your child shares of the business, you have a valuation done on the company that applies discounts to the value of what your child receives. There are two significant discounts:

1. **Lack of control.** Since you're passing only 1 percent of the business to your child at a time, you still have complete control of the company. The IRS considers that 1 percent to be less valuable to the child than its monetary value because he or she can't really do anything with it—your child has no control over the business.

2. **Lack of marketability.** There's no easy way for your child to monetize that 1 percent. He or she can't sell it on the stock exchange or sell it to an investor who might want to buy in to a privately held business. No one is likely to want to buy a 2 percent or 3 percent share in a small business. Since that percentage isn't marketable and therefore is illiquid, a discount applies here as well.

Combined, those two discounts might reduce the value of your gift by 35 percent or so. That means that in the eyes of the IRS, instead of giving your child $100,000 in company stock each year, you're actually transferring only $65,000. So instead of being over the gift tax exclusion by $72,000 per year, you're over it by only $37,000. That preserves more of your estate tax exemption. If you leave the rest of your business to your child after your death, he or she will have a smaller amount on which to pay estate tax.

GRANTOR RETAINED ANNUITY TRUST (GRAT)

Now we get into more complex estate planning tools that are appropriate only for higher-net-worth investors. The grantor retained annuity trust, or GRAT, is one such tool. Savvy financial advisors use it to ensure that future appreciation on liquid assets is realized outside of the taxable estate.

Under a GRAT, a grantor (in this case, you) establishes an *irrevocable trust*—a trust that can be terminated only according to terms specified within the trust or by court order. The grantor then transfers the assets he or she wishes to freeze into the GRAT in exchange for an annuity paid over a specified term. The term can be a fixed number of years (no fewer than two), the remainder of the grantor's life, or the shorter of a fixed number or the grantor's life.

The annuity consists of a portion of the principal plus an implied interest rate set by the government. During the payment term, you as the grantor will receive annuity payments, which can be made no less frequently than annually. At the end of the annuity term, the balance of property remaining in the trust passes to your beneficiaries.

What makes the GRAT useful for estate planning is that it can be "zeroed out" for tax purposes. The annuity amount (a percentage of the initial fair market value of the assets transferred to the trust) is set so that the amount paid to the grantor over the term of annuity is equal to the amount transferred to the GRAT, plus interest. According to federal gift tax laws, at the end of the annuity term, the grantor is considered to have received back everything he or she put into the trust—and thus to have made no taxable gift to the beneficiaries. Any appreciation of the assets remaining in the GRAT can pass to the beneficiaries gift-tax free.

For this reason, the ideal assets for a GRAT tend to be growth-oriented stocks and shares of closely held businesses. Because the annuity payments come either from interest earned on the assets contained in the trust or a percentage of their value, appreciation of such assets has the potential to outpace the value of annuity payments, so the underlying assets don't lose value by the time the trust expires and assets remain to pass on to beneficiaries.

On the other hand, if the assets underperform, there are no negative consequences for the grantor—you get a do-over. This makes the GRAT useful for passing on assets to heirs without incurring the gift tax. However, timing is important: If the donor dies before the trust expires, the assets revert back to his or her taxable estate. The beneficiary receives no tax break.

INTENTIONALLY DEFECTIVE GRANTOR TRUST (IDGT)

Like the GRAT, the intentionally defective grantor trust is an irrevocable trust. What differentiates it from the GRAT is that the IDGT is drafted with a deliberate grantor power, so you as the grantor retain some control over the assets in the trust. This forces you, not the trust, to pay any income tax on trust income. That's why the trust is called "intentionally defective."

Assets transferred into the trust become the property of the trust, and while the gift tax applies when the assets move into the trust, those assets and any appreciation are then excluded from your taxable estate. Because you pay the income tax on the trust's annual earnings, any assets that would typically be used to pay taxes remain in the trust instead. This allows the assets held in trust to grow more, and any earnings that accumulate inside the trust pass to your beneficiaries without estate tax. You as the grantor also retain the right to substitute other property of equal value for the property initially gifted.

Estate planners often use the IDGT to mitigate estate tax on *illiquid assets* (assets that are not easily turned into cash) that are expected to increase in value, such as shares in a closely held business.

IRREVOCABLE LIFE INSURANCE TRUST (ILIT)

Life insurance is one of the most commonly owned financial products in the country. If you have a high income, you may have millions of dollars in life insurance to protect your family. That's a good thing, but when it comes to estate planning, a life insurance payout can become a problem, too.

You see, while life insurance death benefits are not taxable as ordinary income to the beneficiary, the death benefit can be taxable as part of your estate, which could push you over the exemption limit and increase your estate tax burden. The irrevocable life insurance trust, or ILIT, is a way to own a life insurance contract outside of your estate. Upon creation of this irrevocable trust, the trust takes ownership of the grantor's (your) life insurance policy, and the trust terms, which you decided on when the trust was created, will list the beneficiaries and provide specific instructions for the trustee as to how the beneficiaries will receive the life insurance proceeds. Once the trust is established, the grantor cannot have any control over the assets or beneficiaries. If you do, the life insurance will be included back once more in your taxable estate.

Upon your death, the policy held in trust will yield a payout that can be used to offset some or all of the estate tax your heirs incur. The life insurance benefits under this type of trust are also free of income and estate taxes, making this a terrific way to use life insurance.

FAMILY LIMITED PARTNERSHIP (FLP) AND LIMITED LIABILITY COMPANY (LLC)

A family limited partnership is typically used to facilitate the transfer of assets—including ownership in a family business, real estate, public stock, or any other type of investment—from one generation to the next. A family limited partnership operates like any other partnership, but has only family members as partners.

If you put a business in an FLP or a limited liability company (LLC), the *general partners* (who manage the partnership and its assets) can start gifting shares from that collection of assets to the limited partners. FLPs and LLCs are both circumstances where using lack of control and lack of marketability discounts can reduce the value of gifts on the estate tax exemption. FLPs and LLCs also allow family members to pool their financial resources and reduce their legal, accounting, and financial planning costs.

SPECIAL NEEDS TRUST

Special needs trusts, as the name suggests, are designed for beneficiaries who may be mentally or physically disabled. By placing assets in trust, the grantor enables the beneficiary to use the assets while not increasing his or her taxable income in such a way that the beneficiary can no longer receive needs-based government services. Such trusts also allow a trustee to manage the assets on the beneficiary's behalf in the event that he or she lacks the mental capacity to make sound financial or legal decisions.

It should be clear that estate planning is about caring for the people in your life in the future—ensuring that after you're gone, they benefit from your success with minimal difficulty. It's also about making sure that even when you can't speak for yourself due to death or incapacity, your wishes are known and carried out. To reiterate, estate planning should be part of every person's financial plan, especially for the wealthy.

Crossing the Wealth Line

» *You don't have to be an Ultra-High Net Worth investor to enjoy gifting money to your heirs. If, according to your financial plan, it looks as though you will have a surplus of money throughout your lifetime, consider the benefits of gifting to your children now. There's something to be said about the memories that you and your family will create when the gifting happens while you're still around. Work with your advisor to put together a gifting strategy analysis.*

BUILD A WALL AROUND YOUR ASSETS

Insurance is vital. You must have enough insurance to cover your life, home, car, and income in case of disability. But in the case of higher-net-worth individuals, asset protection beyond insurance coverage is extremely important.

But why, you might ask? After all, you can buy enough life insurance to cover your income as long as you qualify medically and financially. Doesn't that mean you can sleep easy? No, not really. Because there are two threats to your wealth that are not protected by insurance: action from creditors and legal liability.

Does being wealthy increase your risk of being sued? According to the Personal Liability Risk Scorecard created by insurance company ACE Private Risk Services, some factors that are common to the wealthy certainly make them more likely to be the target of a personal liability lawsuit.[1] Is your net worth in excess of $2 million? Your risk is higher and rises along with your net worth. Do you own more than one home? Your risk jumps for each property. Do you employ domestic staff? Higher risk. Likewise, if you own a boat or multiple cars, sit on a charitable board, manage a family trust, have rental properties, throw big parties, or are simply well known, your risk of a lawsuit increases.

A 2012 survey of individuals from households with more than $5 million in investable assets conducted by ACE, titled "Targeting the Rich: Liability Lawsuits and the Threat to Families with Emerging and Established Wealth,"[2] asked wealthy individuals if they felt they were at greater risk of liability lawsuits. Nearly 40 percent felt they were more likely to be sued. Yet of the respondents, more than 40 percent carried less than $5 million in umbrella liability insurance. Twenty-one percent had zero umbrella coverage.

If you still harbor doubts that wealth makes you a more likely target for frivolous litigation, consider some of these examples of real umbrella policy liability claims:

» Parents hosted a birthday party for their teenager. They didn't serve alcohol, but some of the guests brought alcoholic beverages. Later, one of the teens who attended the party and had been drinking was in a car accident and was badly hurt. The injured teen's parents filed a lawsuit that blamed the accident on his drinking alcohol at the insureds' home. The court found for the claimant, even though the parents didn't serve the alcohol.

» A sports coach filed a personal injury lawsuit against the parents of a girl who had made several defamatory remarks about the coach online. The coach earned an award of $750,000 against the parents' umbrella policy.

» A man named Richard Overton sued Anheuser-Busch for $10,000 for false advertising when drinking a six-pack of Bud Light did not produce visions of beautiful women on a beach, as the company had portrayed in its advertising. Fortunately for common sense the case was thrown out of court, but it illustrates that when you have money, there is always a risk that someone will try to claim some of it.

Sometimes claims can get pretty ridiculous, especially when the target is a deep-pocketed business. Whether the risk of a lawsuit is real or imaginary, you have a lot to lose. Damages in lawsuits involving serious injury are commonly well in excess of $5 million. You need to protect yourself, and insurance alone won't get it done. You need to work with a team of professionals who can add value by putting asset protection measures in place.

THE TWO THREATS

Before exploring some of those protective tools, let's take a closer look at the twin threats of lawsuits and creditor action. Physicians and others in litigation-heavy professions aren't the only ones who are vulnerable to legal action and potential losses. You don't have to be targeted for your wealth for a legal judgment to take away much of what you've worked so hard to accomplish. Your assets can be attached or garnished for a number of reasons, including filing bankruptcy, going through a contentious divorce, or simply being on the receiving end of a civil suit because someone falls and is injured on your property. If you are perceived as having deep pockets, then you can become a target for a plaintiff and his or her attorney, whether or not the case is justified.

Attorneys who represent wealthy clients back up this perception. According to Jeffrey O'Hara, a partner in the law firm LeClairRyan (as quoted in a white paper produced by RCM&D Assurex Global):

> If you look at the frequency of filings in auto accidents and "slip and fall" cases, there is a greater inclination to file a personal injury or worker's compensation lawsuit when times are economically tough. If the defendant is wealthy, this increases the potential for being hit with a suit. A situation that otherwise might have been viewed as a "nuisance event" by the victim is now seen as offering a potential windfall.

The experience of pro wrestling legend Hulk Hogan illustrates how relying on mainstream insurance can put wealthy individuals at risk. Hogan's teenaged son was engaging in an illegal street race when he crashed, causing his passenger to sustain a serious brain injury. The injured teen's family took Hogan to court, and he quickly reached the $250,000 limit of his auto insurance policy. That left his estimated $30 million personal fortune open to a damaging liability judgment. He ended up settling with the family out of court, but an inexpensive umbrella policy probably would have prevented most of that loss.

The other important threat to your wealth is action by creditors: your ex-spouse in a divorce case, the federal government coming after you for unpaid taxes, lenders and other debtholders in a bankruptcy. Trusts and other instruments can protect assets from creditor claims, but they don't always apply in divorce cases or when the IRS is involved. If you pay your debts and don't foresee a divorce in your future, you may think your threat from creditors is small. But life changes. Smart people prepare for the possibility that things won't always go right.

Being prepared doesn't necessarily mean you can prevent lawsuits or avoid creditors. If you're wealthy, being sued at some point may be inevitable. And if you are sued, you have no control over what a court decides. As for creditors, attempting to hide assets from them can make a bad situation worse. Instead, the goal here is to build a wall around your assets and make as much of your wealth as possible legally *untouchable*. That way, should you come under threat, the potential damage is minimized and you don't lose everything.

UMBRELLA INSURANCE

In building that wall, you can't discount insurance. A lot of people get insurance because they're required by law to have it on their car and home. Some people buy life insurance. But it's important that you don't nickel-and-dime your way along by securing minimal coverage. A good rule of thumb for life insurance is that in order to cover existing debt and maintain your family's lifestyle, your death benefit should be seven to 10 times your annual income. So if you make $300,000 a year, you should probably have about $2.5 million in life insurance.

However, life insurance isn't the only important type of insurance. One of the most important overlooked types of insurance, and one that all higher-net-worth individuals should have, is umbrella liability insurance that wraps over your assets. Umbrella liability coverage is coverage for general liability, those unpredictable occurrences that can easily result in a lawsuit when the other party finds out you're well-off.

For example, let's say you have a 16-year-old son. He's a good driver, but he makes an error in judgment (as kids do) and gets into a car accident. It's nothing serious—just a rear-end job. However, the person in the other car sees you as someone with deep pockets and decides to sue. If you get sued, and you have an umbrella liability policy with $1 million to $2 million in coverage, your assets could have additional protection—at the cost of just a few hundred dollars a year.

For people who have accumulated $5 million or $10 million

in net worth, however, even an umbrella policy is not sufficient protection. That's especially true for business owners, because being in business is inherently litigious. You can be sued easily for everything from copyright infringement to sexual harassment to unfair termination. Physicians face the same risk because of malpractice suits, as do psychologists, financial planners, and attorneys. And umbrella liability policies have limits. For instance, they won't cover business losses or legal claims related to breaches of contract. If you're truly in that higher-net-worth stratosphere, you need something more.

IRREVOCABLE TRUST

An irrevocable trust is one of the best vehicles for protecting a large share of your assets. (Revocable trusts, on the other hand, do not provide asset protection.) An irrevocable trust is an account run by an independent trustee that shields the assets in the trust from most creditors. What many people don't know is that you can receive occasional distributions from your trust if you have a provable need for the funds, such as a healthcare expense, so you're not necessarily cut off from those funds for the rest of your life.

Another kind of trust, an irrevocable life insurance trust, can protect any death benefit that is part of your life insurance coverage from going to your creditors instead of to the intended family members.

These are the requirements for an asset protection trust:

» **It must be irrevocable.** That means that once you establish it, the trust can't be changed or terminated without a court order. When you transfer assets into the trust, you surrender your rights of ownership and control over those assets. Control of the assets passes to the trustee you named in the trust. This is one of the major issues some investors have with such instruments: They worry about giving up their ability to use the assets.

» **It must have an independent trustee.** Your trustee should not be your spouse, a family member, or a close personal friend, because courts will look closely at your trust to determine whether the trustee is simply using the funds in the trust on your behalf. You must relinquish all control.

» **The trust documentation must include a *spendthrift clause*.** This clause prevents litigants from suing the beneficiary of the trust to gain access to the assets within the trust. The assets wouldn't become subject to the beneficiary's creditors until after the assets in the trust were distributed and became the beneficiary's property.

LIMITED LIABILITY COMPANY

The limited liability company is a very popular instrument for protecting assets under the umbrella of a business. Forming an

LLC creates a "pass through" entity that, as the name suggests, limits the liability of the individual owners of the company by placing the assets within the structure of the LLC.

LLCs can be established in each state, and not all states offer the same asset protection levels. The highest levels of protection can be found in Nevada and Delaware, which is why so many companies are registered in those two states. For example, Delaware doesn't tax corporations that are formed there but do not conduct business in the state.

A properly designed LLC (with a well-drafted operating agreement) protects your assets in many ways, but one of the most powerful is also one of the least known. If somebody wins a legal judgment against the LLC and obtains ownership of your shares in the LLC (also known as "stepping into your shoes"), that person cannot take the assets out of the LLC. The court could instead grant a *charging order* against the LLC, which allows the creditor to access the assets of the LLC when those assets are distributed— when members are paid. But there are ways around that.

Here is an example: Let's assume your LLC has some rental real estate that generates $50,000 in income per year. A charging order would give a creditor who won a judgment against you the ability to access the assets of the LLC when they're distributed. So to protect the assets, you don't distribute them. Do you lose access to those funds forever? Not necessarily. Here's the interesting part: Even if the creditor doesn't take possession of the assets, the IRS treats the income generated by the assets as taxable income for the creditor!

So the creditor would have to pay tax on that $50,000 of income, even though they're not receiving it. It's phantom income to them. After a few years of paying tax on income they have never received, many creditors simply give up.

Word of advice: You know those DIY services you hear about so much on the radio, offering to help you set up an LLC online for $199? Don't use them. If you're trying to set up an LLC to protect assets from lawsuits and creditors, talk to an experienced asset protection attorney. Consider setting up your LLC in Nevada or Delaware to take full advantage of their strong asset protection laws. One of the keys to successfully protecting your assets in an LLC is a solid operating agreement, and drafting one takes a good attorney. Believe me, it's worth spending a few thousand dollars to get things done the right way. The result might end up saving you millions.

For example, let's say you live in Florida and you decide to create a do-it-yourself LLC. But because you don't know any better, you charter the LLC not in Nevada or Delaware, but in Florida. Big mistake. A 2010 Florida Supreme Court decision found that a charging order is not the only means a creditor has of accessing the assets in the LLC. Under Florida law, if you are a member of an LLC—whether you're the sole member or there are multiple members—a creditor can seize a membership interest as though it were corporate stock. If you didn't know that, you might find your LLC vulnerable at the worst possible time. The moral of the story: Talk to an attorney who specializes in asset protection.

CASH VALUE LIFE INSURANCE

When most people think about buying life insurance, they think about *term life,* a policy that offers a death benefit for a set period of time, such as 20 years, but accumulates no value. If the policy expires without the benefit having been paid, the insured loses all those premiums. Now, in most cases, financial advisors will recommend that their clients purchase term life because *whole or universal life* insurance is not the best "value" for the money. However, if you need a place to accumulate cash value that's judgment- and creditor-proof, whole or universal life insurance can be a perfect solution.

Whole and universal life policies are permanent, intended to span your entire life as long as the premiums are paid. Both can accumulate cash value that you can borrow against while you're still alive. Whole life premiums remain the same for life; universal life premiums are flexible and give you the option to pay less or more than the target premium. With both types of insurance, the cash value growth is tax-deferred. Additionally, the cash can be accessed on a tax-free basis if the policy is structured properly.

But from an asset protection standpoint, creditors and litigants have no claim on your death benefit unless the insurance policy was designed to pay off creditors. Whole or universal life offers your assets first-class protection from judgments in lawsuits and creditor actions. The laws governing these policies are state-specific, so once again it's worth the time to check with your financial advisor or attorney about how this option works in your state.

RETIREMENT ACCOUNTS

As a higher-net-worth investor, you're probably holding most of your assets in taxable accounts, not in tax-advantaged retirement accounts like an IRA or a 401(k). However, the Employee Retirement Income Security Act of 1974 (ERISA) made certain retirement accounts and employee welfare benefits, such as medical insurance, health savings accounts, and disability benefits, completely or partially off limits to creditors—even to bankruptcy collections agencies. The best-known example of this involved O. J. Simpson. After being found liable in civil court for causing the death of Ronald Goldman in the infamous double murder case, Simpson was allowed to keep his NFL pension.

Under ERISA, the following kinds of retirement accounts are protected from creditors and legal judgments:

» 401(k) (protected from all creditor judgments, including bankruptcy)

» 403(b)

» SIMPLE IRA

» SEP IRA

» Employee stock ownership plan (ESOP)

» Employee profit-sharing plan

» Defined benefit plan such as company pension

Traditional and Roth IRAs are not protected by ERISA. However, they do have some protection. The Supreme Court has ruled that individually directed IRAs have federal protection from bankruptcy judgments up to a current limit of about $1.28 million. Also, rollovers from employer plans into an IRA are protected under ERISA with no limit. Outside of bankruptcy proceedings, IRA protection is state-specific. Inherited IRAs, on the other hand, have no bankruptcy protection.

You may have more than one IRA or Roth IRA account, and you may also have a 401(k). However, this doesn't mean you can simply move exposed assets into a series of retirement accounts. There are strict contribution limits for such accounts. In order to transfer nonqualified assets into an IRA or another protected account, you would need to sell the asset, pay applicable taxes, and then make contributions slowly but surely over the course of several years (if you even qualify). Another important fact to note is that while traditional and Roth IRAs have protection up to only about $1 million, assets "rolled over" into a new IRA that cannot receive additional contributions enjoy an unlimited bankruptcy exemption.

As mentioned earlier, state laws vary, and different accounts may have different protection levels from jurisdiction to jurisdiction. If you want to have confidence in the asset protection power of these plans with regards to your situation, get good financial counseling.

TAKING PRECAUTIONS WITH YOUR ASSETS

As with most things in finance, beneficial action starts with consulting the right experts. Once you've done that, follow these commonsense suggestions to ensure that you protect your assets in the most effective way possible without running afoul of the law:

» **Plan before there's a claim.** You can't buy insurance *after* you get sick and then expect your coverage to be valid. Likewise, you can't put asset protection plans in place after you get sued or creditors come after you, and then expect your plan to protect you. The time to create trusts, buy umbrella insurance, or shelter assets in an LLC is before a claim or liability appears. A good advisor will recommend this because when you've accumulated significant wealth, minimizing risks to that wealth becomes an important and intentional part of your overall financial plan. Trying to protect assets after a claim appears could cause you to run afoul of "fraudulent transfer" laws and have your protective measures nullified by a court.

» **Start a separate LLC for your investments.** Investors view LLCs and corporations as entities that are intended only to hold business assets, and there are good reasons not to commingle personal and business assets in the same LLC. For example, if you mix personal assets into your business entity, a creditor may be able to gain access to those assets by claiming that the business is merely functioning as your alter ego. However, starting a separate LLC to hold personal investments is a sound protective strategy.

» **Update your insurance.** Asset protection is vital, but so is insurance. For one thing, an asset protection strategy won't pay your legal expenses if you're sued; some insurance policies will. Depending on your profession, talk to your insurance agent about updating your professional insurance and adding or increasing your umbrella liability policy. That way, you'll have maximum protection against threats ranging from business lawsuits to personal injury claims.

» **Don't try to hide assets.** It's extremely difficult to conceal assets from a court or creditors, and it's almost always illegal. Attempting to keep assets secret, or not disclosing assets in a bankruptcy or divorce proceeding, will only make matters worse—potentially taking you from a scenario where you're merely losing assets to creditors to one where you're being charged with perjury or fraud. Take proactive measures to protect yourself and your beneficiaries, and then be as transparent as the law requires.

Most important of all, even if you have a financial advisor you trust, spend some time with an attorney who is both familiar with the laws of your state and an expert in the asset protection field. This is a very specialized field of law that, for maximum protection, requires first-class advice. Nobody knows better than an asset protection attorney the laws that can affect you, and no one is better equipped to keep you on the right side of the law.

Crossing the Wealth Line

» *Max out your umbrella insurance. You don't have to have $10 million in assets to be at risk of a major liability judgment should something unfortunate happen.*

» *Set up LLCs for your investment accounts with rock-solid, well-constructed operating agreements.*

CREATE WIN-WINS FOR YOU AND YOUR FAVORITE CHARITIES

According to Giving USA, Americans donated an estimated $373.25 billion to charity in 2015. Individuals gave the bulk of that money, $264.58 billion, with the balance coming from foundations, charitable bequests, and corporate giving. And a substantial portion of those individual gifts came from wealthy individuals, especially rich, young high-tech entrepreneurs flush with Silicon Valley dollars.[1]

You may have seen stories claiming that America's wealthy have been giving a lower percentage of their incomes to charity in the past few years, but those are misleading. In fact, charitable giving among families with a net worth of at least $1 million or an annual income of at least $200,000 increased 28 percent from 2011 to 2013, according to "The 2016 U.S. Trust Study of High Net Worth Philanthropy" by private bank U.S. Trust and the Indiana University Lilly Family School of Philanthropy. Incomes for those families are increasing, so they are actually donating a smaller percentage of their incomes. But make no mistake: The wealthy are generous.

If you decide to pursue philanthropic giving, proper planning by experts will ensure that not only you but the community receives the greatest possible benefit from your generosity. In 2015, Facebook founder Mark Zuckerberg and his wife, Dr. Priscilla Chan, announced that they were transferring 99 percent of their Facebook stock—worth about $45 billion at the time—into a charitable LLC called the Chan Zuckerberg Initiative. Its stated purpose was "to join people across the world to advance human potential and promote equality for all children in the next generation."

Zuckerberg and Chan received criticism from some quarters that their plan was more about avoiding taxes than about charitable giving, but the intent seems clear. While Zuckerberg's charitable plan may be extreme, it was certainly put together with quite a bit of planning to ensure maximum benefit for both him and the charity. He earned his money legally and through a great deal of hard work and innovation, and he's under no obligation to give a cent to charity. Since he and his wife are choosing to do so, why shouldn't they also take advantage of everything in the tax code that saves them money now and confers additional benefits to their heirs?

Being wealthy can come with criticism, even when you're trying to do good and give to causes that you care about. But don't shy away from working with your professional team to create a charitable giving plan that also benefits your interests. That's not gaming the system; that's wise.

CUTTING A CHECK IS NOT ALWAYS BEST

It's admirable to give to support charitable causes that are important to you. Recent research even shows that charitable giving and generosity can help you live longer and healthier. But you might not be giving in a way that's best for your financial well-being.

Not everyone has to be an idealist when it comes to charitable giving. There's nothing wrong with getting a financial benefit while you support the nonprofit, arts organization, or hospital of your choice. Because of that, cutting a check may not be the best way to support your favorite charitable cause.

If you are already donating to charity, you'd probably like to continue. Aside from the tax deduction, charitable giving can be an important part of a higher-net-worth individual's standing in the community and can lead to social and business connections. Of course, it also allows you to use some of what you've accumulated to give back and help others, which can be incredibly rewarding. Fortunately, there are many alternatives to simply writing a check: You can donate appreciated assets. You can set up different charitable remainder trusts. You can create a donor-advised fund or establish your own private foundation. A solid advisory team can use these tools to help you accomplish charitable goals while providing you with tax benefits.

DEDUCTION LIMITS

However, before getting into some of the specific instruments, we should spend a few minutes talking about the limitations on charitable giving. Contrary to what some people think, you can't give an unlimited amount and simply deduct that from your taxable income.

The amount of a donation that you can deduct from your personal income taxes depends in part on the type of assets you donate and the type of organization to which you donate. Your deduction is also limited by your adjusted gross income (AGI). For example, if you contribute cash to a charitable organization, you can deduct only up to 50 percent of your AGI in the year you make the donation. This table, courtesy of Northern Trust, illustrates the different aspects of the charitable income tax deduction:[2]

Transfer To	AGI Limitation	Deduction Based On
Public charity	50% for cash 30% for long-term capital gain property	Fair market value
Private foundation	30% for cash 20% for long-term capital gain property	Fair market value for cash and publicly traded long-term appreciated securities; tax cost for other long-term capital gain property, including closely held stock and real estate
Charitable remainder trust with public charity as remainder beneficiary	50% for cash 30% for long-term capital gain property	Fair market value
Charitable remainder trust with private foundation as remainder beneficiary	30% for cash 20% for long-term capital gain property	Fair market value for cash and publicly traded long-term appreciated securities; tax cost for other long-term capital gain property, including closely held stock and real estate
Supporting organization	50% for cash 30% for long-term capital gain property	Fair market value
Nonqualified charitable trust	N/A	N/A

Here are some examples of deduction limits in various scenarios:

» Jill has an AGI of $300,000, and she gives $50,000 to the United Way. Her deduction limit is 50 percent of her AGI, or $150,000, so she can deduct her entire contribution.

» Let's say that Jill instead gives $250,000 to the United Way. She can deduct $150,000 for the tax year in which she gives the gift, but what about the remaining $100,000 deduction? The tax code includes a "carry forward" provision that allows a gift amount over the AGI ceiling to be carried forward for up to five years. So Jill can use that $100,000 to reduce her future taxable income as needed.

» What if Jill wants to donate cash to a private foundation such as the Bill & Melinda Gates Foundation? In that case, her deduction would be limited to 30 percent of her AGI, or $90,000. If she gave $50,000 to the foundation, she could deduct her entire gift. If she gave $250,000, she would have to carry over $160,000 ($250,000–$90,000) to future tax years.

GIVING APPRECIATED ASSETS

The donation of stocks, bonds, and mutual funds tends to increase when markets are up, because wealthy investors know that it's a terrific way to make substantial charitable gifts while also getting advantageous tax treatment. For example, Fidelity Charitable Gift Fund reported that in 2014—a year that saw the S&P 500 jump more than 11 percent—57 percent of donated assets consisted of appreciated stock, a 14 percent increase from 2013.[3]

Appreciated assets are assets that have realized an increase in value over at least one year of ownership. It's one of the most tax-efficient ways to give. Instead of selling the asset, paying the capital gains tax, and then donating the remaining cash to charity, you donate ownership of the asset itself. In other words, you're giving 100-cent dollars rather than 76-cent dollars. Keep in mind, though, that your tax deduction cannot exceed 30 percent of your AGI.

For example, Jill owns $100,000 in Apple stock that she purchased for $50,000 five years ago. Keep in mind, Jill is in the highest marginal federal income tax bracket with a long-term capital gains tax rate of 20 percent. Rather than sell the stock and pay long-term capital gains tax on the $50,000 appreciation, she donates the stock to the endowment of a local museum. Because her AGI is $300,000, she can deduct $90,000 of the stock's fair market value of $100,000. Meanwhile, the endowment can sell the appreciated shares without incurring any capital gains taxes. This table shows the advantages for Jill (in terms of potential tax savings and net charitable impact) of donating appreciated assets versus selling an asset and donating the cash:

	Option 1: Donate securities directly to charity	Option 2: Sell securities and donate cash
Current fair market value of securities donated	$100,000	$100,000
Donor's capital gain on asset	$50,000	$50,000

Continued

Long-term capital gains and Medicare surtax, totaling 23.8%	$0	$11,900
Net charitable donation	$100,000	$88,100 ($100,000–$11,900)
Charitable deduction (cannot exceed 30% of the donor's AGI)	$90,000 in year 1; $10,000 in year 2	$88,100
Tax value of charitable deduction (deduction x 39.6)	$39,600	$34,887
Net charitable impact: Tax savings plus total money received by charity	$139,600	$122,987

CHARITABLE GIFT ANNUITY

The goal of an annuity is to provide a steady, annual (hence the name) stream of income. A charitable gift annuity establishes an irrevocable contract between you, the donor, and a charity, whereby you transfer cash or property to the charity in return for a partial tax deduction and a fixed annual payment to a recipient (the *annuitant*) for the rest of that person's life. When the annuitant (usually, but not always, the donor) dies, the charity keeps the gift and payments cease. Gift annuities are often part of the charitable giving programs for universities, arts organizations, hospitals, and religious organizations.

You can transfer cash, securities, real estate, or shares in a closely held business (and, depending on the charitable organization, possibly other kinds of property) to a charity as part of a charitable gift annuity. The payments you can earn will vary based on a number of factors: the value of the donated asset; the number of annuitants and their ages; and the gift annuity rate the charity offers, which will usually reflect American Council on Gift Annuities guidelines. But in general, this is a good option when interest rates are high, because charities will increase their payment rates to keep their annuities competitive with other financial products.

What about the tax consequences? Deduction rules depend on whether you donate cash (50 percent) or capital gain property (30 percent). In general, your deduction will be the value of the donation minus the present value of the expected payments to be made in the annuitant's lifetime. As for the annuity payments received, the payments will likely consist of a combination of tax-free return of principal, ordinary income, and potentially long-term capital gains. Now you're getting into actuarial tables and the like, so it's best to talk to a tax professional about the tax advantages of a charitable gift annuity. But for investors in retirement who seek tax savings and predictable payments, this can be a valid option.

Here is an example: Howard, age 72, makes a $200,000 cash donation to a university endowment on March 1, 2017, in exchange for a charitable gift annuity. The university invests the gift and, based on the American Council on Gift Annuities guidelines, Howard receives an annual payment of $10,800 from the charity for the rest of his life. According to actuarial tables, the present value of his annuity payments is $108,000. So for his 2017 tax returns, he will get a charitable tax deduction equal to $200,000 minus $108,000, or $92,000.

CHARITABLE REMAINDER TRUST (CRT)

A charitable remainder trust, or CRT, is an irrevocable trust that's typically funded with highly appreciated property such as stocks, mutual funds, shares of a private business, or real estate. A CRT has a current beneficiary (either the donor or a named individual) and a remainder beneficiary—a qualified charity like a private foundation or a public 501(c)(3) organization. Like the charitable gift annuity, it generates an income stream for you or your beneficiaries.

The annuity can be paid annually or more frequently, and the total value of those payments can range from 5 percent to 50 percent of the total fair market value of the assets held in trust, valued in different ways depending on the type of CRT you create. When the donor dies, the charity gets the *remainder* of assets in the trust. The charity can also be one of the beneficiaries, giving it (along with the donor) a predictable income stream. Like gift annuities, CRTs are also favorable when interest rates are high—an important distinction in a low-rate environment.

Charitable remainder trusts are ideal for use by higher-net-worth individuals who want to donate highly appreciated assets such as stocks without incurring a capital gains tax debt. In years when you have higher-than-normal income—such as when you've sold your business or a piece of real estate for a significant gain—creating a CRT can provide you with a one-time income tax deduction while also ensuring a regular stream of income for the future. The current-year deduction is based on the value of the contributed property minus the present value of the estimated annuity payments. So the deduction will be higher or lower depending on the taxpayer's chosen annuity return.

Transferring assets prior to selling them is a great way to defer gains. Instead of paying 100 percent of the gain in the year of sale, the taxpayer pays a small portion of the gain over the term of the trust.

CHARITABLE LEAD TRUST (CLT)

A charitable lead trust, or CLT, is essentially a charitable remainder trust in reverse. The charity receives an income stream in the form of interest income earned by the assets in the trust. At the end of the specified trust term (which can be a set term of years, the lifetime of the donor, or the lifetimes of the donor and the donor's spouse) any income and principal remaining in the trust can either revert back to the donor or pass to other noncharitable beneficiaries named in the trust.

The way CLTs provide tax savings depends on how the trust is structured. There are two options: a *grantor trust*, in which the person who funds the trust pays taxes on the income the trust earns, and a *nongrantor trust*, in which the trust pays the income taxes on those earnings. If you create a grantor CLT, you pay tax on the income but also get an immediate, one-time charitable deduction based on the present value of the future income stream, which can vary depending on what kind of charity is the trust's beneficiary. Like the charitable remainder trust, that makes the CLT a useful tax minimization tool in a year when you're expecting higher-than-normal income.

With a nongrantor CLT, the trust pays income tax each year and gives you an annual income tax charitable deduction. This can be beneficial for high-income investors who aren't expecting their income to be significantly higher than normal in the year of the contribution. The other great benefit of the CLT is that it reduces the size of your taxable estate, because the gift is reduced by the income stream paid to the charity.

When it comes to interest rates, the CLT is the opposite of the CRT: It's most suitable when interest rates are low (as they are in 2017). This is especially true with a grantor trust, which reduces the size of the grantor's estate. With lower rates, the income earned by the trust is lower, so the grantee charity still gets the money but you have less income to pay tax. Additionally, the lower the interest rates are, the higher the present value calculation is for the stream of payments to the charitable beneficiary. That leads to a larger charitable deduction for you.

PRIVATE FOUNDATION

Thanks in part to the many, many high-profile charitable foundations created by ultra-wealthy individuals—the Bill & Melinda Gates Foundation may come to mind—private foundations are one of the most popular, prestigious techniques that the wealthy use to give to charity while gaining some tax and estate planning benefits. According to Explore Foundation Research, in 2014 there were 86,192 private foundations in the U.S. with $715 billion in assets, distributing $52 billion via charitable giving that year.[4] That's more than the GDP of Lebanon. Private foundations are their own economy.

One of the big upsides of the private foundation is its prestige and visibility. A foundation creates a long-term family legacy that can last for many decades. For example, the Rockefeller Foundation was started in 1913, and as of the end of 2015 it was the 41st largest U.S. foundation with more than $150 billion in total giving. A private foundation can keep your family's name relevant long after you're gone. Also, setting up a private foundation lets you keep control over its charitable giving and also fund causes that are meaningful to you.

The downside is that foundations are not as strong as other

tools for tax minimization. True, assets placed in the trust are not taxable as long as the trust is established for one of the following purposes: charitable, religious, educational, scientific, literary, public safety, amateur sports, or preventing cruelty to children or animals. However, other provisions make foundations less ideal as tax havens.

For example, the income tax deduction for most assets placed in the foundation is based on their cost basis—what you paid to acquire them—and not their fair market value, so your deduction is smaller. Foundations are also subject to excise taxes of 1 percent to 2 percent on their net investment income, which can include capital gains, interest, dividends, and similar sources.

Another downside is that private foundations can be costly to set up and administer. Setup requires the assistance of an attorney, and other services that can be expensive. As for ongoing administration, the IRS mandates that a private foundation must spend a minimum of 5 percent of its assets on total charitable expenses, including operating costs, per year. The Council on Foundations recommends that smaller foundations assume they will spend about 15 percent of their charitable budget on administration.

Private foundations are expensive to run and involve many administrative costs, so individuals who start them commonly do so with at least $5 million in assets. So let's say you have a $5 million private foundation. If you adhere to the IRS's 5 percent minimum, you would spend $250,000 per year on charitable expenses. Based on the 15 percent figure for administrative costs, you could expect to spend about $37,500 on legal and accounting services and other costs. Over 25 years, that adds up.

DONOR-ADVISED FUND (DAF)

A donor-advised fund, or DAF, allows you to contribute assets (cash, stocks, real estate, etc.) to a special fund account where the assets are invested tax-free, and you can "advise" the fund manager to release funds to a charity in the future. When you make a charitable contribution to a DAF, you choose your advisors and any successors or charitable beneficiaries. You receive an immediate income tax deduction for the fair market value of the assets, up to 50 percent of your adjusted gross income or 30 percent for long-term appreciated assets, which can be invested and can grow tax-free within the fund. Once you contribute to a DAF, you do not technically own or control the assets anymore, which is why you are allowed to receive the upfront charitable deduction.

A DAF is less expensive to run than a private foundation, and it's less time-consuming because you're running a financial account, not a nonprofit organization. The DAF does carry the disadvantage that it can only give to IRS-qualified public charities.

Consider the different characteristics of private foundations versus DAFs:

	Donor-Advised Funds	Private Foundations
Start-up time	Immediate	Can take several weeks or months
Start-up costs	None	Legal (and other) fees are typically substantial
Ongoing administrative and management fees	85 basis points (0.85%) or less, plus investment management fees	Can be in the range of 250–400 basis points (2.5% to 4% per year)
Tax deduction limits for gifts of cash	50% of adjusted gross income	30% of adjusted gross income
Tax deduction limits for gifts of stock or real property	30% of adjusted gross income	20% of adjusted gross income
Valuation of gifts	Fair market value	Fair market value for publicly traded stock, cost basis for all other gifts, including gifts of closely held stock or real property
Required grant distribution	None	Must expend 5% of net asset value annually, regardless of how much the assets earn
Excise taxes	None	1% to 2% of net investment income annually
Privacy	Names of individual donors kept confidential (if desired); grants can be made anonymously	Must file detailed and public tax returns on grants, investment fees, trustee names, staff salaries, etc.
Administrative responsibilities	Recommend grants to favorite charitable causes	Manage assets, keep records, select charities, administer grants, file state and federal tax returns, maintain board minutes, etc.

One option offers simplicity but anonymity; the other requires more time and money, but allows your name to live on long after you check out of this world. If you're charitably inclined, it's important to plan properly so you select the appropriate charitable strategy given your intentions.

Crossing the Wealth Line

» *If your wealth has grown to the point where you're considering making substantial donations to charity, do your homework. Make sure the charities you're considering are legal charitable organizations and are well run. Visit the websites GuideStar, CharityNavigator, or CharityWatch for overviews of an organization's financial health and history.*

DON'T SELL YOUR BUSINESS YOURSELF

While not everyone reading this book owns a business, a high percentage of higher-net-worth individuals have accumulated their wealth through business ownership. According to CEG Worldwide and Wealth Engine, 33.3 percent of Middle-Class Millionaires own their own businesses or have experienced a liquidity event from a business. That number ratchets up to 74.5 percent for the High Net Worth group and to 89.9 percent for the Ultra-High Net Worth group.[1]

Furthermore, Merrill Lynch estimates that 80 percent of people with at least $5 million of investable assets are former business owners who have had a successful exit. Beyond that, about half of all Americans with a net worth of $1 million or more earned their wealth by growing a business. So the odds are good that even if you don't own a business, someone close to you does.[2] The take-away: If owning a business is a clear path to building wealth, selling the business is what makes that wealth a reality.

Because of this, the sale of your business is a critical, probably once-in-a-lifetime event. You might be depending on the proceeds of that sale to fund your retirement. You may want to sell the business to your employees or your beneficiaries so it will continue to be run according to your values. In any case, your business is probably your most valuable asset, and selling it is not a do-it-yourself project. Unfortunately, too many business owners tell themselves that because they were able to build a profitable company in engineering, manufacturing, technology, or any other sector, they have what it takes to sell their business, too.

Don't make that mistake. As with just about everything in the world of finance, selling a business is far more complex than it might appear, and hiring a professional—an investment banker—to help you do it right is worth far more than anything you might pay that person. In fact, choosing to work with an investment banker might be the best financial decision you will ever make.

WHAT INVESTMENT BANKERS DO

Among the many reasons for seeking the advice of an investment banker, the most obvious one is this: Whereas you will probably sell only one business in your life—the one you started—experienced investment bankers have sold dozens if not *hundreds* of businesses.

They know how to help you get your company in shape to demand the highest possible price, how to find qualified buyers, and how to negotiate the best deal with the best terms. In short, they're experts who are unlikely to stumble over complicated financial matters or make irreversible financial mistakes.

First of all, what is an investment banker? Forget what you might be thinking about Gordon Gecko or any other fictional Wall Street characters. In this context, an investment banker is a financial professional who works at a financial institution that specializes in helping public and private companies raise capital and that advises company owners on mergers and acquisitions. Investment bankers are also experts in effectively selling small businesses.

What do investment bankers do to help business owners? It's a long list:

» Provide an initial valuation of your business, so you know what your company is worth and can set realistic expectations.

» Identify the potential market of buyers for your company, and promote your company to a pool of qualified buyers.

» Recommend strategies that can increase the market value of your company and thus your final sale price. This could potentially mean pushing back your sale by a year or more, but if it nets you an extra few million dollars, it's probably worth it.

» Weed out the serious prospective buyers from the tire kickers.

» Maintain confidentiality throughout your transaction.

» Hold and manage a competitive auction that increases your sale price and pairs you with the best possible buyer for your company.

» Negotiate your best possible deal, taking things like tax implications into account.

» Ensure a smooth, timely closing.

AVOID IRREVERSIBLE MISTAKES

Most important (and most often overlooked), your investment banker can keep you from making irreversible mistakes in what will probably be the most important financial transaction of your life. Some business owners make the mistake of assuming that because they're good at running their business, they'll be good at selling it, too. But while you might be an expert at growing and operating a business, are you an expert at selling one? Not likely. Selling a business is tricky. The stakes are high, and getting all the value out of what you've built is *not* a DIY project.

The fact is, being an expert in one thing does not make you an expert in everything related to it. For example, back around 2000, Tiger Woods was at his peak—the best golfer on the planet, winning 14 major tournaments. But even then, he had Butch Harmon, his legendary swing coach, who constantly tinkered with Tiger's approach in order to keep him at the top of his game. Experts need help. Tiger was an expert at golf, but he still needed somebody on the outside looking in to identify areas for improvement.

In 2011, after going through his very public divorce and suffering some injuries, Tiger let his longtime caddie, Steve Williams, go. The loss of Williams, long regarded as one of the game's best caddies, had an immediate impact. From 2011 through 2015, Tiger won only eight tournaments, compared with 18 from 2007 to 2009. Expertise matters, both in golf and when you're selling a business.

A THOUSAND HOURS

Another reason an investment banker is invaluable is that it takes a great deal of time to properly sell a business. The typical merger and acquisition (M&A) process takes about 1,000 man-hours and six to nine months to complete. Do you have that kind of extra time to spend, on top of the time you spend running your business? You probably don't. But your investment banker will.

A thousand hours might seem excessive, but there is a lot more to selling a business than first meets the eye. Here's how the process typically goes:

1. **Your investment banker works with you to learn everything about your company and your industry.** He or she might spend months reviewing your internal processes and systems, interviewing your management team, looking at the

growth curve in your market, investigating current M&A trends, and looking at recent transactions in your industry and the multiples that similar companies are selling for. The goal is to learn what makes your company valuable while identifying possible issues that could affect your price or "sellability" and to correct as many of those issues as possible. For example, your banker determines that while your company has a number of long-term clients under contract and a healthy cash flow, its management and operational strategy resides largely in your brain. Unless you plan to stay on after selling, that reduces the value of the business, because the buyer would need to reinvent the company's operational methodology from the ground up and risk losing customers in the process. This is likely to reduce your sale price or multiple. In such a case, your banker would probably recommend that you and your senior team codify everything you know about running the business in written form and turn it into a series of replicable processes and systems. That way, anyone purchasing the company could step into a leadership role and, in a short time, learn how to run the business with the least amount of disruption for customers, employees, and profits. This would likely enhance your sale price or multiple.

2. **With the business optimized, your investment banker provides you with a professional valuation of your business.** In reading and talking to people, you might hear a lot of speculative numbers thrown around, but the bottom line is this: *Your business is worth what a buyer will pay.* Getting

an accurate valuation will allow you to determine whether your value expectations are realistic and whether the money you will net from the sale fits with your financial goals. Ultimately, this information may (or may not) compel you to proceed with the sale of your business.

3. **If you decide to proceed with a sale, your banker creates promotional materials,** such as a confidential information memorandum (CIM), designed to generate interest from buyers.

4. **Your banker reaches out to prospective buyers using his or her contacts in industry and finance.** Interested buyers will receive a broad overview of your company without confidential details, such as the company name. Only those that sign a confidentiality agreement will gain access to more sensitive, confidential information.

5. **Your banker sets a deadline by which interested buyers must submit an indication of interest (IOI)—a basic proposal to buy your business.** Each IOI contains a valuation range: a range of what your business might be worth to the buyer in a sale. With this information, you and your banker begin narrowing the field to the best prospective buyers.

6. **After picking the best three to five buyers, you and your banker develop a management presentation to highlight the value drivers of your business.** Then comes your first chance to meet the prospects. Prospective buyers who submit high-quality IOIs (those that include high valuations,

attractive terms, and lots of detail) may also get access to more of the inner workings of your company, including financials and trade secrets.

7. **Buyers who like what they see are asked to submit a letter of intent (LOI).** These documents will contain a specific offer for your business, the proposed deal structure, desired conditions (such as the founder remaining with the company for a term after the sale), and other details.

8. **Your investment banker works with you to determine which offer has the most merit.** Once you choose your buyer, your banker will negotiate specific terms in the LOI to maximize value for you. He or she may also bring in other experts such as tax attorneys to ensure that details such as the tax implications of your sale are addressed. The buyer and seller then sign the LOI, which provides the road map for the purchase agreement and other closing documents.

9. **The buyer executes the due diligence process, investigating everything about your business.** These diligence items will become a part of the purchase agreement and will also become the seller's legal representations of the state of the business. Assuming the buyer doesn't find anything that compels them to either kill or request changes to the deal, the drafting of the purchase agreement will proceed. Finally, any open issues with the business or the deal are addressed, documents are signed, and the sale closes.

It's your investment banker's job to herd all these cats, keep everything proceeding in a timely manner, ensure that all buyers comply with confidentiality and disclosure standards, and help you get your business ready to be sold. Most important, working with a competent and qualified investment banker throughout this process will prevent you from making irreparable financial mistakes. Selling a business is not a do-it-yourself affair.

STUBBORN MISCONCEPTIONS

Despite all this, there are still business owners who stubbornly hold on to misconceptions about it being a good idea for them to sell their own business. Let's put these misconceptions to rest:

» **"I can sell the company myself."** You built your business, so who better to sell it than you? The trouble is that besides the time-consuming process of finding, vetting, and negotiating with buyers, the sale of a business is a very complicated transaction. Your entire future in retirement might hinge on getting the price you hope for, and if you mess up the deal, you don't get a second bite at the apple.

» **"I don't want to pay the investment banker's fee."** This shows the same lack of understanding that leads some people to go "For Sale By Owner" with their home instead of hiring a Realtor because they don't want to pay the commission. How much is your time worth? Probably a lot more than the 1 percent to 5 percent fee you might pay your investment banker. (The fee is based on the size and complexity of the deal and is typically based on something called the "Lehman Schedule.") The fact is, investment bankers almost always provide value that exceeds their fee by putting more money in your pocket. They're also experienced deal makers who will protect you from pitfalls, such as accepting *earnouts* (contractual provisions that guarantee you additional compensation in the future if the business reaches certain financial goals) instead of a cash deal, or signing an unfavorable noncompete agreement.

» **"I've already found the buyer. Why would I pay the investment banker?"** First of all, you may not end up doing business with that specific buyer. In fact, that happens quite often. Sometimes, what looks like an ideal buyer at first isn't your best choice. But apart from that, wouldn't you rather have multiple parties bidding on your business and driving up the price? Also, is money your only goal in the deal, or are there potentially other factors that make a deal desirable, such as ensuring that your employees still have jobs after you leave? Furthermore, investment bankers do a lot more than simply line up buyers. Out of the typical 24-week process, an investment banker will usually spend only about four weeks looking for buyers. While that's a very important part of the process, it's less than 20 percent of the total workload involved. And let's be honest, if you end up working with the buyer you found, don't you want him to put his best foot forward?

Here's what can happen without an investment banker at the helm: A business owner with a company that was doing $5 million in annual EBITDA then sold it for a multiple of five—$25 million. Great, right? It seemed that way, but when the owner was asked if he had used an investment banker, he said that he didn't have to; the buyer had approached him. Unfortunately, he was informed, investment bankers had regularly been selling healthy companies like his in the same industry for multiples of seven or eight through a controlled auction process that gets prospective buyers to put their best foot forward.

The owner's jaw hit the floor. He began doing the math in his head. If his company had sold for a multiple of eight times EBITDA, his final sale price would've been $40 million. Typically, investment banking fees can range from 2 percent to 5 percent on a deal of that size, but even after paying an investment banking fee of 5 percent—$2 million—he would've netted $38 million. That's quite a premium! Don't be penny-wise and pound-foolish.

Finding the buyer is only part of what an investment banker does. His or her main job is to run a process that finds the right buyer who pays the right price and gives you a successful exit.

PLANNING FOR A SUCCESSFUL SALE

It bears repeating: Selling your business will probably be the most important financial event of your life. Done right, it can fund a dream retirement, help you pass real wealth on to your kids, enable you to take care of your employees, and give you the funds to build a legacy. But it's not as easy as running an ad on eBay. Here are some of the important steps you should be taking even if your exit is years away.

» **Start planning for your exit now, before you're preparing to sell.** Buyers want well-run, well-built businesses with sustainable cash flows and strong growth potential. Those things don't happen by accident. They happen because foresighted owners grow their businesses with their exit in mind early on. Cleaning up your books, formalizing management methods and business practices, hiring good people, investing in the best technology—none of that happens on the fly after you decide to sell. It happens years in advance, so do what you can to get started today.

» **Get a proper valuation of your company now, and decide what you need to net from the sale.** That's how you know the kind of number you need to shoot for. Let's say you want to walk away from the sale of your company with $20 million before taxes. Your EBITDA is $4 million a year, but a valuation tells you that companies like yours are selling for about three times EBITDA. That's $12 million—$8 million short of your goal. Now you know you've got some work to do: Either grow your business or take whatever steps are required to make it worth a higher multiple.

» **Hire the right person to do your valuation.** You could spend $10,000 to hire a CPA who's also a Certified Valuation

Analyst, but you don't need to go quite that far. You can get an accurate *open market valuation* by hiring an experienced M&A advisor or CFP® professional for considerably less. Valuing your company requires an expert with the experience and skills to take the changing variables into account. Do *not* rely on online valuation calculators or back-of-the-envelope valuation techniques.

» **Know how to increase your company's sale price.** If your valuation doesn't return a number you can live with, then you need to increase either your company's EBITDA or its potential multiple. Increasing EBITDA is about growth and profitability, so how can you expand and increase revenues while decreasing expenses? As for increasing your multiple, anything that makes your business appear less risky to a buyer will help.

Develop revenue sources that recur over time, such as long-term service contracts. Build a diverse customer base; companies that generate more than 15 percent of their revenues from one customer make buyers *very* nervous. Maintain clean financial statements in accordance with generally accepted accounting principles, or GAAP. Build a strong management team that can operate independently of you. Be transparent about expenses, especially what you take out of the company to pay for your lifestyle. Document all your systems and processes in exhaustive detail so that a new ownership team could get up and running with little or no downtime.

» **Know whether you prefer an external or an internal transfer.** An *external transfer* is a sale to a third party. You'll probably get cash and/or buyer equity, and in some cases you may be asked to stay on in a consulting role for a limited time. An *internal transfer* happens when you sell the business to your management team or an employee team, typically through either a management buyout (MBO) or an employee stock ownership plan (ESOP). Internal transfers often involve seller financing, and you rarely get a large amount of cash at closing. Instead, the sale price is paid over time, which can give you a long-term income stream and spread out the tax obligation from the sale. However, without receiving as much cash at closing, you bear more risk. An MBO is a strong option because it offers a smooth transition after the sale, reducing risk and keeping business and cash flowing. Meanwhile, ESOPs come with significant tax advantages.

» **Know whether you really want to pass your business to your children.** It's entirely understandable why business owners want to do this—continuity, leaving a legacy, family pride, and so forth—but you should proceed with caution on this option. The reality of selling a business to your kids is that it will almost always involve risky seller financing, so your children will have to run the business profitably in order for you to get all your money. In my experience, it's very rare for children to have the same passion for or interest in their parent's business, so they often end up doing a poor job of running it. When these situations don't work, they have the potential to disrupt family dynamics. Nobody wins. Better options include creating a family limited partnership, or selling to a third party and then giving your children a meaningful financial gift.

» **Know whether the final price is your only goal.** Is a big payout all you want from your sale? There's nothing wrong with that, of course; you're selling your business to net as much money as possible. But perhaps the final check is not the only important thing in your transaction. For example, do you want to start a new company in the same industry? Then you'd better be cautious about noncompete clauses in your contract. Do you want to remain involved in the company you built, or ensure that your loyal managers and employees will be taken care of after you leave? Build it into your deal. Is your buyer asking you to accept earnouts in order to meet your price? You'd better make sure the terms are fair and realistic, or you might never see your full sale price. Know what you want before you sell.

» **Know the tax consequences of selling.** For example, if your business is an S corporation, an LLC, or a sole proprietorship, it's considered a "pass through" entity and you can sell assets to another party and pay capital gains tax on that sale. But if it's a C corporation, you could be subject to double taxation in an asset sale. There's not much you can do to change that (unless you own a time machine), but you should be prepared in advance for the tax implications. Selling assets or stock, allocation of the purchase price—many aspects of your sale can have a significant impact on your tax liability. Discuss them in advance with your financial advisor, tax attorney or CPA, and investment banker.

» **Know how your sale affects your Family Index Number.** Remember the FIN? That's the annualized return you need on your investments in order to reach your family's goals. Obviously, the sale of your business will affect that number. When you build the net proceeds from your liquidity event into your plan, are you comfortable with your adjusted FIN? Can you realize that annualized return through the implementation of a prudent investment strategy? If it appears that you'll still need to swing hard for a home run after your liquidity event, you should rethink the plausibility of your exit. On the other hand, if your FIN is at a level that permits you to take an easy swing when you step up to the plate, proceed with confidence.

» **Know how selling changes your financial road map.** If you are a higher-net-worth individual, your business is almost certainly your largest and most important asset, so selling it changes everything about your financial future. Your financial road map should change at the same time, and you need to make sure you have a financial advisor who can handle your plan both before and after the sale. For example, before the sale is when you should make decisions that will affect your tax liability after the sale. After the deal closes and you pay applicable taxes, you will probably be sitting on a large amount of cash. What will you do with it? Give some to your beneficiaries? Endow a charitable foundation? Purchase commercial real estate? How will those decisions impact your current portfolio? For most people, selling a business is a once-in-a-lifetime windfall, and you need a road map to make sure the sale and its aftermath are enjoyable and fruitful.

That brings me to the emotional, lifestyle-oriented side of selling. Many business owners don't consider this side of things until after the ink on the paperwork is dry. Then they feel depressed, lost, and unhappy. You see, if you've spent 25 years building a business, it's a big part of your life. It's a part of who you are. Before you sell your business, ask yourself how you'll feel when you're not getting up in the morning, driving to the office, seeing old friends and acquaintances, and solving problems.

Not running your business anymore also dramatically impacts your lifestyle. What will you do with your time? Do you have a plan? Are you the kind of person who can play golf five days a week and be happy, or do you crave challenge? If you want to start another business, can you start one in the same industry, or will you be bound by a noncompete? These questions matter just as much as the financial ones. Because in the end, selling your business should make you happy. If it doesn't, maybe it's not time to sell.

One final suggestion: If you're thinking about selling your

business in the next five years, here's your chance to complete a free Sellability Score analysis, which you can find at https://swpconnect.com/free-sellability-score. It will provide you with a Sellability Score ranging from 1 to 100. A score above 80 means your business will likely sell at a multiple that's above average for companies similar to yours. A score from 50 to 80 means your company should yield an average multiple. And anything below 50 means that your business is likely to sell at a below-average multiple—or not sell at all—unless you put in some smart work to make it more saleable. No matter what your score is, it's good information to have if you own a business.

Crossing the Wealth Line

» *Your business might be too small for a full merger and acquisition process. What about a management buyout? Look for a successor, and find a way for that person to begin buying you out. Consider an ESOP. It can give you an opportunity to monetize a portion of the business as long as your cash flow is strong.*

» *Accumulate assets outside of your business. Plan for the worst-case scenario—that your business doesn't have enough value to be saleable and to contribute meaningfully to your financial plan.*

» *Consider investing in qualified retirement plans outside of your 401(k), like a cash balance plan.*

» *Get a professional valuation of your business so you know where you stand today.*

» *Talk to an investment banker or other professional with experience in valuing businesses to get ideas for growing the value of your company so you can exit profitably.*

YOU'RE NOT HIRING A FINANCIAL ADVISOR— YOU'RE HIRING A LIFETIME FINANCIAL PARTNER

Your personal physician. Your attorney. Your first professional mentor. Your financial advisor. There are few people who have as much impact on the outcome of your adult life than those four, and out of all of them, your financial advisor is arguably the most pivotal. Consider the reasoning behind this.

Your physician helps you maintain good health as the years pass and steers you toward good lifestyle choices. Most people are relatively healthy for decades, however, and illness doesn't really impact their daily lives. Your lawyer helps you be prepared for the unexpected and deal with legal threats, but of course, you hope you'll never need that. Your mentor may have shaped your entire career path but doesn't affect your life now. But your financial advisor impacts your wealth, and your wealth affects every decision you make, from healthcare to legal services to starting, running, or selling a business.

Where you live, whom you know, whom you trust, how you play—your wealth affects all of it. And no one is a greater influence on that wealth than your advisor. So the choice of who to trust in building your financial strategy is one of the most critical choices you will ever make in your adult life, period.

Back in 2015, a financial wellness educator and attorney named Erik Carter wrote a terrific, brave article in *Forbes* titled "Confessions of a Former Financial Advisor: 5 Things I Didn't Tell My Clients." In the piece, he confessed to engaging in practices early in his career that, while not illegal, were not in his clients' best interests. This is part of what Carter wrote:

> I was only paid to sell certain products or gather assets. If I didn't recommend that clients invest in our products or use our services, I didn't eat. However, that didn't stop me from advising clients to build up an emergency fund, pay off high-interest debt, and max out their employer's retirement accounts before investing with me. (I can't say that was true for all advisors though.)

The one exception was IRA rollovers, which are the bread-and-butter for many advisors. This is despite the fact that there are many reasons why you might be better off rolling your previous employer's retirement plan into your current one or even leaving it where it is rather than rolling it into an IRA. Similarly, I neglected to tell clients about other alternatives to my firm's products like direct-sold insurance policies, no-load mutual funds, U.S. government savings bonds, prepaid college plans, and investing directly in a real estate property or business. I also rarely if ever discussed strategies to improve and protect my clients' credit scores; deal with student loans, mortgages, and other debts; buy a home; get their estate planning documents in order; or address a host of other important financial decisions that didn't involve selling investment or insurance products.

Carter didn't want to compromise his values anymore, so he left the profession altogether. But the point of Carter's confession is not to imply that all financial advisors think of themselves before their clients. That's not necessarily so. Instead, the point is to demonstrate how easy it is for an investor who doesn't ask enough questions to wind up working with someone who's doing *some* of what's required for the investor's financial welfare, but not all.

In other words, just as you can't assume that someone who has a medical degree is a competent physician, you also can't assume that someone who has CFP® or CFA after his or her name is automatically a financial and investments whiz with only your well-being in mind. Selecting an advisor is a hugely important decision, and you need to know what to look for and what questions to ask in choosing that professional. Your decision will be critical to not only your prosperity but that of your family.

YOUR FINANCIAL PARTNER

You would think this would be obvious to the wealthy, who spend so much of their time either accumulating substantial assets or spending them, but it's not. According to Investopedia, more than one-third of investors with at least $30 million in investable assets are DIY investors who don't work with financial advisors.[1] According to the same survey, another 23 percent of the wealthy consult a financial advisor only about complex investments. So more than half of the very wealthy are not getting the kind of holistic financial wisdom and guidance that could help them reach their goals in multiple areas of their lives.

That's a mistake, and it needs to be corrected. Just about any person of wealth can benefit from working with a properly credentialed, ethical, experienced financial professional. That's not opinion; it's fact, supported by data like the Vanguard findings shared earlier that show how a good financial advisor can add *about* 3 percent annually to a client's net return over the lifetime of the relationship. The figure below shows how Vanguard arrived at that roughly 3 percent number:[2]

Vanguard Advisor's Alpha Strategy	Module	Typical Value Added for Client (basis points)
Suitable asset allocation using broadly diversified funds/ETFs	I	>0bps*
Cost-effective implmentation (expsense ratios)	II	40 bps
Rebalancing	III	35 bps
Behavioral coaching	IV	150 bps
Asset location	V	0 to 75 bps
Spending strategy (withdrawal order)	VI	0 to 110 bps
Total-return versus income investing	VII	>0bps*
Total potential value added		About 3% in net returns

*Value is deemed significant but too unique to each investor to quantify

Vanguard's research identifies five key practices that a financial advisor should follow in order to deliver that kind of value:

1. **Be a good behavioral coach.** Helping clients stay cool-headed, avoid panic decisions, practice financial discipline, and keep a long-term perspective on the markets is potentially worth 1.5 percent of that 3 percent.

2. **Apply an asset location strategy.** Properly balancing assets between taxable and tax-advantaged accounts is shown to be worth up to 0.75 percent in additional value.

3. **Develop a client spending strategy.** Once retirement arrives and clients begin to take distributions from their accounts, a smart spending strategy can help them minimize tax obligations by withdrawing funds from the right accounts and by properly investing untouched funds. This can add as much as 1.1 percent.

4. **Employ cost-effective investments.** Finding ways to reduce clients' fees and other expenses can have a significant impact on net returns, adding up to 0.4 percent.

5. **Systematically rebalance assets.** Effective advisors regularly rebalance their clients' assets within various asset classes to maintain the desired blend of risk and performance. A systematic rebalancing strategy ensures that portfolios remain optimized for risk/return while employing an automated process for buying low and selling high. This can potentially add 0.35 percent to that 3 percent total.

A qualified, experienced, dependable financial advisor who can be counted on to put your needs first is a lot more than a stock jockey. He or she will be your financial quarterback and partner—someone who can help develop holistic solutions for every part of your life.

DIFFERENT FINANCIAL ADVISORS

However, the truth of that doesn't necessarily make it easier to choose the financial advisor who's best for you. For one thing, the financial world comes with an alphabet soup of professional designations. What do they mean, and which one is best for your situation?

» **CERTIFIED FINANCIAL PLANNER**™ **practitioner (CFP® professional).** CFP® professionals undergo the most stringent training of anyone in the financial planning world. To earn the designation, they must pass a rigorous certification exam covering insurance, investments, taxation, employee benefits, retirement, and estate planning, administered by the CFP® Board. CFP® professionals must also meet strict standards for ethics and conduct. They are the gold standard in comprehensive financial planning.

» **Chartered Financial Analyst (CFA).** The CFA charterholder is an investment specialist, highly skilled in portfolio management, asset allocation, and investment analysis. Charterholders go through extremely stringent training to earn their certification, and they must pass three exams, each of which requires at least six months of study and coursework, and accumulate at least four years of approved work experience. They are the gold standard in portfolio management.

» **Certified public accountant (CPA).** CPAs are the gold standard in accounting—the experts in issues involving taxes. CPAs must complete 150 hours of education, have no less than two years of public accounting experience, and pass the difficult Uniform Certified Public Accountant Examination, which is set by the American Institute of Certified Public Accountants (AICPA) and administered by the National Association of State Boards of Accountancy (NASBA).

The optimal financial services solution for higher-net-worth investors would include a team consisting of each of these professionals, along with an attorney skilled in such areas as tax and estate planning law. Such an arrangement offers a comprehensive range of crucial services, from portfolio management and asset allocation to tax planning, legal services, and the implementation of a long-term financial strategy.

A multifaceted team also gives you access to unique investment opportunities like private equity and hedge funds and helps you integrate value enhancers such as tax minimization, estate planning, and charitable giving into your overall financial plan.

HOW IS YOUR ADVISOR COMPENSATED?

Another issue to consider is how your financial advisory team is compensated. In the past, the most common compensation model was the commission. Financial advisors would collect a commission each time they sold an asset in a client's portfolio. As you might expect, this created conflicts of interest. An advisor trying to increase his or her income might have a high volume of turnover in a client's portfolio, regularly buying and selling stocks, bonds, and mutual funds. Sometimes the company selling the financial products would pay the commission, but sometimes the client would pay. Of course, this activity might also hurt the performance of clients' investments. It really wasn't an ideal model, and today it's outdated.

For some years now, the industry has been switching over to a fee-based compensation model. Fee-based advisors cannot collect commissions on any investment product. Instead they can be paid on an hourly basis, receive a fixed annual retainer, or receive a percentage of assets under management (AUM). The percentage of AUM model is the most common and most popular compensation plan, because it aligns the advisor's interests with the client's. Your advisor typically earns around 1 percent of the total value of the assets he or she manages; if your portfolio under management has a current value of $2 million and your advisor's fee is 1 percent, then you're paying $20,000 per year for financial services.

This is advantageous because if the value of your assets grows, your advisor's compensation grows as well, providing an additional incentive for your professional team to work to increase your wealth. Some advisors also receive a percentage of profits— hedge fund managers, for example, who commonly receive 20 percent of the increase in the investment's value over a specified period of time. Though that may seem high, aligning an advisor's financial interests with those of his or her clients makes for a strong and effective business model. For this reason, as well as the obvious reasons of transparency and ethics, fee-based compensation is superior to commission-based compensation.

A FULL-SERVICE SOLUTION

Let's say you have a very high net worth—$50 million in investable assets, for example—and an extremely busy life. You're running a business or a company as a top executive. You're constantly traveling for work. Your spouse and other family members are equally busy. Because you have multiple homes and investments, your finances are complex. You need more than portfolio management or tax planning. You need full-service wealth management that makes your life easier.

Enter the multi-family office (MFO), a solution for the elite individual who needs comprehensive financial management from a single source. While a single-family office (SFO) might take care of one ultra-wealthy family, an MFO delivers end-to-end wealth management to a group of select higher-net-worth families.

There are about 3,500 family offices around the country. They provide standard wealth management functions from asset allocation to estate planning, but also offer a soup-to-nuts financial solution that might include tax compliance work, access to private banking and private trust services, document management and recordkeeping services, expense management, budgeting, insurance, managing charitable giving, advice to family-owned businesses, estate planning, bill paying, bookkeeping services, family member financial education, family support services, and family governance.

In other words, family offices provide everything you might need, under one roof. Not many higher-net-worth families will need the services of an MFO, but if you find yourself working with numerous independent financial practitioners to get needed services and experiencing chaos, an MFO can be a lifesaver, bringing order and a smooth ride.

The professional and personal services of an MFO don't come cheap. In some cases, you'll pay separate fees for each profession under the MFO umbrella: CFP® professional, attorney, CPA, and CFA charterholder. However, if it means ending the chaos and having one entity that can get your *entire financial life* under control . . . well, let's just say that for a lot of folks, it's worth it.

CHOOSING THE RIGHT QUARTERBACK

As in football, success begins with the field leader—the quarterback. In financial services, that's your financial advisor. Finding that professional should be your first goal. The key is to find an advisor who's on your side of the table, working for the same cause.

It should be someone who has your best interests in mind. You want someone who's fully transparent about fees and costs and who's free of any conflicts of interest. Don't work with a pseudo-financial advisor who is really a closet insurance salesman. Here are some key questions to ask in choosing your advisor:

» **"How are you compensated?"** You want a fee-based advisor. Find out what percentage of assets under management the advisor receives and at what intervals.

» **"What certification do you hold, and how often do you do continuing education to stay current?"** A CFP® professional or CFA charterholder is your best choice, because these professionals receive the most stringent training.

» **"What services does your firm provide?"** Ideally, you want a practice that provides tax planning, estate planning, portfolio management, and accounting and legal services—either all under one roof or using a team of trusted partners at different locations.

» **"How do you provide value?"** This is an important question, because the answer will tell you how well the advisor understands the difference he or she makes for clients. Savvy advisors know that their greatest impact is not in picking stocks but in managing investor behavior—and, in the case of higher-net-worth clients who have already locked up their retirement, reducing volatility and giving them a smoother ride.

» **"What is your investment philosophy?"** You should be working with someone whose approach to risk and personal values are similar to your own. That way, you'll both be on the same page when it comes to taking care of what's most important in your life.

» **"Can I speak to some of your clients?"** Get referrals. Speak with past and current clients, and find out whether what they say about the advisor matches up with what the advisor is telling you.

Those referrals matter; pay attention to them. Your advisor should be someone of good character, because someone who's honest and ethical will do what's in your best interest even if it's not always in his or her best interest. We trust our financial advisors not just with our money but with our family's future. That means being vigilant, asking a lot of questions, and checking credentials.

One example of the risks of choosing the wrong advisor comes from the *American Greed* TV show on CNBC. Scott Rothstein was a Fort Lauderdale, Florida, lawyer determined to build the biggest, best law firm in the state. But how to raise the capital to build it? He decided to set up a complex Ponzi scheme, purchasing fabricated "structured settlements," where people sell large settlements in legal cases for lump sums of cash. But the settlements in question didn't exist, and Rothstein paid his promised 15 percent returns to his investors out of the cash he got from later investors.

Eventually, the $1.2 billion scam (one of the largest in history) fell apart, and in 2009 Rothstein turned himself in to authorities. But his victims lost hundreds of millions of dollars—though they were some of the lucky ones, eventually receiving $363 million in restitution. Many victims of financial scams never recover a cent.

Remember, if an investment or financial return seems too good to be true, it probably is.

A financial advisor worth considering will not sell you with unrealistic claims. He or she will promote a measured, realistic, multifaceted financial strategy intended to get you to your goals steadily over time, needing no home runs and avoiding strikeouts.

MAKING YOUR LIFE BETTER

The role of the financial advisor has changed. Just as the Internet has helped patients become highly informed before they walk into their doctor's offices—and just as it has turned Aunt Judy into a de facto travel agent—it's helped a lot of people become, if not investment experts, at least more knowledgeable about financial markets and investment products.

Thanks to CNBC, *Kiplinger's*, and more, there's a ton of data out there, and even more so-called experts who can offer you advice on the next big stock. However, quality advisors create real value by keeping their clients from making bad decisions during times of volatility, creating smart asset allocation models, advising clients against bad investments, helping minimize tax obligations, and ensuring that sound records are kept. In other words, a great financial advisor doesn't just make your investments better; he or she makes your *life* better.

As you know, there are many perks to affluence. You don't have the day-to-day financial worries of people with lower income or even those of the Middle-Class Millionaire. You have opportunities to live an incredible lifestyle and make a real difference for your children and the world. But wealth comes with its challenges, and one of those challenges is realizing that, while you don't face the same financial obstacles as other people, you still face obstacles.

That's where the financial advisor provides his or her most valuable products: perspective and peace of mind. Because what good is wealth if you're too busy worrying about a lawsuit or an IRS audit to enjoy it? The right financial advisor will be someone who doesn't just understand your financial needs but understands *you*. He or she will get to know your values, goals, anxieties, fears, dreams, and passions and will develop a solution that serves all those aspects of your life, not just your net rate of return. The right advisor can make life better in so many ways:

- » **Minimizing fear.** You will spend less time worrying about likely and unlikely threats, from market downturns and legal judgments to letters from the IRS and actions from demanding creditors.

- » **Giving you more freedom.** Feeling like you always have to be watching your investment accounts can restrict your freedom to travel, enjoy your favorite activities, and really live your life. Sound financial management can free you of those concerns.

- » **Taking care of your family.** You've worked hard to give your family an amazing lifestyle and financial security. The right advisor can help you further protect them with everything from estate planning to college savings.

» **Managing your business to sell.** The businesses that sell for the highest multiples start making sale-based decisions years before they seek to sell. Your advisory team will help you build a business that nets you the highest possible price and, when you're ready to sell, connect you with a top investment banker.

» **Giving you more time.** Wealth costs time. The more you have, the more time you probably spend away from your home and family earning it. Now that you're wealthy, it's time to spend less time managing your assets and more time enjoying them. Your advisor will help you do that.

» **Giving you a smooth ride.** Peace of mind is the ultimate luxury. When you know that you have an optimal portfolio, a sound tax strategy, moderate risk, and strong legal and financial representation behind you, you have peace of mind. You know things are taken care of, and even if the markets hit a bump, you're going to be okay. That's a great feeling.

Your financial advisor should be someone who does more than manage your portfolio. He or she should be a friend, confidante, and mentor. You're a part of an elite segment of the financial world. Be sure to work with people as elite as you are—who can help you use the wealth keys and unlock the full potential of your assets and hard work.

Crossing the Wealth Line

» *Find a financial advisor who recognizes the importance of planning. The advisor should have a proactive process for updating your plan throughout the relationship. If the advisor says he or she will set up a plan for you only when you're a new client and after that upon request, continue looking.*

» *Don't assume all financial advisors are cut from the same cloth. Do your homework, and ask plenty of questions.*

» *Most important, partner with a skilled advisor as soon as possible. Finding the right financial advisor or team is one of the best ways to maximize your chances of embracing the higher-net-worth world.*

CONCLUSION: THINGS TO REMEMBER

In closing, remember that your needs aren't like everyone else's. You're a higher-net-worth investor. Your situation is more complex than the average person's. The advice you see and read in the mainstream media—the advice aimed at people with less than $1 million in investable assets—is not geared toward you. To optimize your wealth and give your family the brightest possible future, you should consider the sophisticated strategies I've laid out here. Here are some key things for higher-net-worth individuals to remember:

- » Wealth management, not just portfolio management, is essential.

- » Success means more than asset performance. It means reduced volatility and a smooth ride, so you can not only build wealth but enjoy it.

» Your financial advisor should also be your point person for risk management, tax minimization, asset protection, wealth transfer, charitable giving, and coordinating professional relationships between members of your wealth management team.

I hope the information provided here has helped you see things more clearly and clarify the path forward. What should you do next? I recommend getting an assessment of where you are today in your wealth building journey. You can do that in less than 15 minutes at www.wealthalyze.com. After answering a series of questions, you will receive a score ranging from 0 to 100 that shows you how well you're moving toward optimizing your wealth:

» A score of 90 or better means your plan is first-class and may need only a few tweaks.

» A score between 70 and 90 means you should probably get a second opinion from a financial advisor to see how you can repair any leaks in your boat.

» A score below 70 means there is significant room for improvement in your wealth management strategy.

I hope you will take the assessment and get the guidance you need to live the life you deserve. Whatever you do, I thank you for your time and wish you health, wealth, and wisdom.

Mark Tepper, CFP®

NOTES

Introduction

1   Net Worth By Age Percentile Rank Calculator, Shnugi Personal Finance, http://www.shnugi.com/networth-percentile-calculator/

2   UBS, "What is Wealthy?" UBS Investor Watch, Q3 2013

3   Media kit, Kiplinger's Personal Finance

4   Source: 2016 Spring GfK MRI

Key #1

1   Dave Ramsey and Sharon Ramsey. (2003). *Financial Peace Revisited.* Harmondsworth, Middlesex, England: Viking Penguin. p. 325. 0-670-03208-5.

2   Peter Kuhn, Fernando Lozano, "The Expanding Workweek? Understanding Trends in Long Work Hours Among U.S. Men, 1979-2004," NBER Working Paper No. 11895, The National Bureau of Economic Research, December 2005.

3   http://www.philanthropyroundtable.org/almanac/statistics/

4 Kyle Pomerleau, "An Overview of Pass-through Businesses in the United States," Tax Foundation, January 21, 2015, https://taxfoundation.org/overview-pass-through-businesses-united-states/

Key #2

1 Thomas Corley, "16 Rich Habits," *Success*, September 8, 2016, http://www.success.com/article/16-rich-habits

2 Francis M. Kinniry Jr., CFA, Colleen M. Jaconetti, CPA, CFP ®, Michael A. DiJoseph, CFA, Yan Zilbering, and Donald G. Bennyhoff, CFA, "Putting a value on your value: Quantifying Vanguard Advisor's Alpha," Vanguard research, September 2016, https://www.vanguard.com/pdf/ISGQVAA.pdf

Key #3

1 Pablo S. Torre, "How (and Why) Athletes Go Broke," *Sports Illustrated*, March 23, 2009.

2 Genworth 2016 Cost of Care Survey, conducted by CareScout, May 2016.

3 "S&P 500: Total and Inflation-Adjusted Historical Returns," Simple Stock Investing, http://www.simplestockinvesting.com/SP500-historical-real-total-returns.htm

Key #4

1 Steven Goldberg, "What I Learned From Sequoia Fund's Tragic Love Affair With Valeant," *Kiplinger's*, April 29, 2016, http://www.kiplinger.com/article/investing/T041-C007-S001-sequoia-fund-s-tragic-love-affair-with-valeant.html

2 S&P 500 Return Calculator, with Dividend Reinvestment, https://dqydj.com/sp-500-return-calculator/

3   Francis M. Kinniry Jr., CFA, Colleen M. Jaconetti, CPA, CFP®, Michael A. DiJoseph, CFA, Yan Zilbering, and Donald G. Bennyhoff, CFA, "Putting a value on your value: Quantifying Vanguard Advisor's Alpha," Vanguard research, September 2016, https://www.vanguard.com/pdf/ISGQVAA.pdf

4   D. Kahneman and A. Tversky. (1984). "Choices, Values, and Frames." *American Psychologist*. 39 (4): 341–350. doi:10.1037/0003-066x.39.4.341.

5   B. De Martino, D. Kumaran, B. Seymour, and R. J. Dolan. (2016). "Frames, Biases, and Rational Decision-Making in the Human Brain." *Science* (New York, NY). 313(5787):684-687.

6   "The Impact of Taxes on Investor Returns," *Philosophical Economics,* December 20, 2015, http://www.philosophicaleconomics.com/2015/12/taxes/

Key #5

1   Ben Carlson, "Peter Lynch's Track Record Revisited," *A Wealth of Common Sense,* July 17, 2016, http://awealthofcommonsense.com/2016/07/peter-lynchs-track-record-revisited/

2   John Reeves, "Insights for investors from a founding father of behavioral finance," *USA Today,* August 8, 2015, http://www.usatoday.com/story/money/personalfinance/2015/08/07/insights-founding-father-behavioral-finance-motley-fool/31191537/

3   Francis M. Kinniry Jr., CFA, Colleen M. Jaconetti, CPA, CFP®, Michael A. DiJoseph, CFA, Yan Zilbering, and Donald G. Bennyhoff, CFA, "Putting a value on your value: Quantifying Vanguard Advisor's Alpha," Vanguard research, September 2016, https://www.vanguard.com/pdf/ISGQVAA.pdf

4   Jilian Mincer and Steven C. Johnson, "Insight: Mom and pop investors miss out on stock market gains," *Reuters,* September 30, 2012, http://www.reuters.com/article/us-usa-stocks-retailinvestors-idUSBRE88T0AE20120930

5   Russell Kinnel, "Mind the Gap 2014," *Morningstar,* February 27, 2014, http://news.morningstar.com/articlenet/article.aspx?id=637022

6 "INVESTING AND EMOTIONS: The Ups and Downs of the Market," BlackRock, https://www.blackrock.com/investing/literature/investor-education/investing-and-emotions-one-pager-va-us.pdf

7 "Principles for successful long-term investing," JPMorgan Chase & Co., https://am.jpmorgan.com/blob-gim/1383387362150/83456/MI-FB-PRINCIPLES_Q416_r2.pdf

8 S&P 500 Dividend Reinvestment and Periodic Investment Calculator, https://dqydj.com/sp-500-dividend-reinvestment-and-periodic-investment-calculator/

9 Nathaniel Popper, "After Facebook, More Fear of Stock Market," *New York Times,* May 28, 2012, http://www.nytimes.com/2012/05/29/business/retreat-from-stock-market-continues.html

10 Jilian Mincer and Steven C. Johnson, "Insight: Mom and pop investors miss out on stock market gains," *Reuters,* September 30, 2012, http://www.reuters.com/article/us-usa-stocks-retailinvestors-idUSBRE88T0AE20120930

11 ibid.

12 Sam Ro, "CHART OF THE DAY: How A Few Poorly-Timed Trades Can Torpedo Two Decades Of Healthy Returns," *Business Insider,* March 24, 2014, http://www.businessinsider.com/cost-of-missing-10-best-days-in-sp-500-2014-3

13 Alexandra Twin, "Geithner talk gooses stocks," *CNN Money,* November 21, 2008, http://money.cnn.com/2008/11/21/markets/markets_newyork/

14 Kent Daniel and David Hirshleifer. "Overconfident Investors, Predictable Returns, and Excessive Trading." (2015). *Journal of Economic Perspectives.* 29(4):61–88.

15 Barber, Brad M., and Terrance Odean. (2000). "Trading is Hazardous to Your Wealth: The Common Stock Investment Performance of Individual Investors." *Journal of Finance* 55(2): 773–806.

16 "The case for Vanguard active management: Solving the low-cost/top-talent paradox?" Vanguard Research, January 2013, http://www.vanguard.com/pdf/s356.pdf

17 Rick Ferri, "Any Monkey Can Beat The Market," *Forbes,* December 20, 2012, https://www.forbes.com/sites/rickferri/2012/12/20/any-monkey-can-beat-the-market/#704add02630a

18 Brad M. Barber and Terrance Odean. (2001). "Boys Will Be Boys: Gender, Overconfidence, and Common Stock Investment." *Quarterly Journal of Economics* 116(1): 261–92.

19 Anne Jones Dorn, Daniel Dorn, and Paul Sengmueller. (2014). "Trading as Gambling." *Management Science* 61(10): 2376-2393.

20 Brad M. Barber and Terrance Odean. (2008). "All That Glitters: The Effect of Attention and News on the Buying Behavior of Individual and Institutional Investors." *The Review of Financial Studies* 21(2).

21 Ravi Dhar and Ning Zhu. (2006). "Up Close and Personal: Investor Sophistication and the Disposition Effect." *Management Science* 52(5): 726-740.

Key #6

1 Chris Farrell, "Listen to Warren Buffett and embrace low-cost index funds," *Minneapolis Star Tribune,* May 7, 2016, http://www.startribune.com/listen-to-warren-buffett-and-embrace-low-cost-index-funds/378349261/

2 Speech, "Remarks by Chairman Alan Greenspan, at the Annual Dinner and Francis Boyer Lecture of The American Enterprise Institute for Public Policy Research, Washington, D.C.," December 5, 1996, https://www.federalreserve.gov/boarddocs/speeches/1996/19961205.htm

3 Editorial, "'The Superinvestors of Graham & Doddsville' Buffett's 1984 speech," *Kenyan Wall Street,* January 10, 2017, http://kenyanwallstreet.com/buffetts-speech-at-columbia-business-school-in-1984-the-superinvestors-of-graham-doddsville

4 Anders Bylund, "How Hewlett-Packard Stock Nearly Doubled In 2013," *The Motley Fool,* December 30, 2013, https://www.fool.com/investing/general/2013/12/30/how-hewlett-packard-stock-nearly-doubled-in-2013.aspx

5 "Value vs. Glamour: A Long-Term Worldwide Perspective," The Brandes Institute, February 2015

6 Malcolm Baker, Brendan Bradley, and Jeffrey Wurgler, "Benchmarks as Limits to Arbitrage: Understanding the Low-Volatility Anomaly." *Financial Analysts Journal* 67(1).

7 S&P 500 Return Calculator, with Dividend Reinvestment, https://dqydj.com/sp-500-return-calculator/

8 Ned Davis Research analysis of companies underlying the Russell 3000 Index, a measure of the broad U.S. equities market. Data is from February 2, 1987 through December 31, 2015.

9 John Buckingham, "The Compelling Case For Dividend Paying Stocks," *Forbes,* May 1, 2015, https://www.forbes.com/sites/johnbuckingham/2015/05/01/the-compelling-case-for-dividend-paying-stocks/#6bfcb952725d

10 Kevin McDevitt, "The S&P 500 Remains Relevant at 60," *Morningstar Advisor,* March 6, 2017, http://www.morningstar.com/advisor/t/118093139/nominees-for-2016-domestic-stock-fund-manager-of-the-year.htm?pageid=566037

Key #7

1 Kimberly Amadeo, "Fed Funds Rate History: Highs, Lows and Chart With Major Events," *The Balance,* February 8, 2017, https://www.thebalance.com/fed-funds-rate-history-highs-lows-3306135

2 http://www.multpl.com/10-year-treasury-rate/table/by-year

3 http://www.multpl.com

4 http://www.multpl.com/10-year-treasury-rate/table/by-year

5 http://www.multpl.com

6 Thomas Kenny, "Stocks and Bonds, Calendar Year Performance," *The Balance,* August 3, 2016, https://www.thebalance.com/stocks-and-bonds-calendar-year-performance-1980-2013-417028

7 "The Behavior Gap: Buy High, Sell Low," Keating Wealth Management, Q2 2016

8 Michael Mackenzie, "Complacency is number one enemy of this ageing US credit cycle," *Financial Times,* October 17, 2016, https://www.ft.com/content/56cdd6ac-9454-11e6-a80e-bcd69f323a8b

9 ibid.

10 Leo Benedictus, "Burritos, cheese and Bowie: curious bonds and unusual investments," *The Guardian,* February 7, 2016, https://www.theguardian.com/business/shortcuts/2016/feb/07/burritos-cheese-and-bowie-curious-bonds-and-unusual-investments

11 Sean Hanlon, "Bonds Are Boring, Right?," *Forbes,* December 3, 2014, https://www.forbes.com/sites/advisor/2014/12/03/bonds-are-boring-right/#849dcc72971f

Key #8

1 "Long-Term Capital Management – LTCM," Investopedia, http://www.investopedia.com/terms/l/longtermcapital.asp

2 Michael Lewis, "Betting on the Blind Side," *Vanity Fair,* April 2010.

3 Morningstar, "2016 Fundamentals for Investors," http://home.mp.morningstar.com/elabsLinks/FundamentalsForInvestors_2016.pdf

4 ibid.

Key #9

1 Dan Mitchell, "The Tax System Explained in Beer," *International Liberty,* March 18, 2012, https://danieljmitchell.wordpress.com/2012/03/18/the-tax-system-explained-in-beer/

2 https://www.irs.gov/uac/newsroom/net-investment-income-tax-faqs

Key #11

1 Personal Liability Risk Scorecard, ACE Private Risk Services, 2012

2 White paper, "Targeting the Rich: Liability Lawsuits and the Threat to Families with Emerging and Established Wealth," ACE Private Risk Services, 2012

Key #12

1 Giving USA 2016: The Annual Report on Philanthropy for the Year 2015, Giving USA

2 "Income Tax Charitable Deduction Summary," Insights on Wealth Planning, Northern Trust 2014

3 "2015 Giving Report," Fidelity Charitable

4 http://foundationcenter.org/gain-knowledge/foundation-research

Key #13

1 John J. Bowen Jr., Paul Brunswick, James Dean & Jonathan J. Powell, "The State of the Affluent 2014," CEG Worldwide, LLC, 2014

2 Thomas J. Stanley and William D. Danko Marietta, (1996). *The Millionaire Next Door*. GA: Longstreet Press, Inc.

Key #14

1 "Ultra High Net Worth Individual (UHNWI)," Investopedia, http://www. investopedia.com/terms/u/ultra-high-net-worth-individuals-uhnwi.asp

2 Francis M. Kinniry Jr., CFA, Colleen M. Jaconetti, CPA, CFP *, Michael A. DiJoseph, CFA, Yan Zilbering, and Donald G. Bennyhoff, CFA, "Putting a value on your value: Quantifying Vanguard Advisor's Alpha," Vanguard research, September 2016, https://www.vanguard.com/pdf/ISGQVAA.pdf

INDEX

ABOUT THE AUTHOR

Mark Tepper is the president and CEO of Strategic Wealth Partners, a comprehensive wealth management firm that specializes in working with higher-net-worth families. Strategic Wealth Partners has made the Inc. 5000 for several consecutive years, making it one of the fastest-growing private companies in America. Mark has helped his clients develop and oversee their financial plans, prudently manage their investment portfolios, and facilitate successful exits from their privately held businesses.

A well-known financial commentator, Mark appears regularly on CNBC's *Power Lunch* and *Closing Bell* as well as on the Fox Business Network. He has been featured in the *Wall Street Journal*, *Kiplinger's*, and *Inc.* magazine. Mark is also a member of Entrepreneurs' Organization (EO).

Mark holds a BSBA in finance from John Carroll University and is a CERTIFIED FINANCIAL PLANNER™ professional. He lives in Richfield, Ohio, with his wife, Jamie; his daughters, Cameran and Riley; his son, Kellen; and their two dogs. In his free time, he is passionate about softball, golf, and high-performance driving.